WAR, ECONOMY AND THE MILITARY MIND

War, Economy and the Military Mind

Edited by
GEOFFREY BEST
ANDREW WHEATCROFT

CROOM HELM
ROWMAN AND LITTLEFIELD

First published 1976
Copyright © 1976 Croom Helm Ltd
Croom Helm Ltd, 2-10 St John's Road, London SW11
ISBN   0 85664 229 0

First published in the United States 1976
by Rowman and Littlefield, Totowa, New Jersey

Library of Congress Cataloging in Publication Data
Main entry under title:
War, economy and the military mind.
  Includes bibliographical references.
  1. Armies – History – Addresses, essays, lectures.
2. Navies – History – Addresses, essays, lectures.
3. War – Addresses, essays, lectures. 4. Munitions –
History – Addresses, essays, lectures. I. Best, Geoffrey
Francis Andrew. II. Wheatcroft, Andrew.
UA15.W37 1976   355.3'09   75-19119
ISBN 0-97471-759-4

Printed and bound in Great Britain by
REDWOOD BURN LIMITED
Trowbridge and Esher

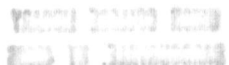

CONTENTS

Acknowledgements

Introduction

Part 1	1
1 Regimental Ideology *John Keegan*	3
2 Pre-revolutionary Army Life in Russian Literature *Richard Luckett*	19
3 Making an Army Revolutionary: France 1815-48 *Douglas Porch*	32
4 Technology and the Military Mind: Austria 1866-1914 *Andrew Wheatcroft*	45
Part 2	59
5 Naval Armaments and Social Crisis: Germany Before 1914 *Volker Berghahn*	61
6 The British Armaments Industry 1890-1914: False Legend and True Utility *Clive Trebilcock*	89
7 Organising an Economy for War: the Russian Shell Shortage 1914-17 *Norman Stone*	108
8 How Right is Might? Some Aspects of the International Debate about How to Fight Wars and How to Win Them, 1870-1918 *Geoffrey Best*	120
Notes on Contributors	136

ACKNOWLEDGEMENTS

The editors wish to express their gratitude to the Nuffield Foundation, which with great generosity financed the conference at Edinburgh University entitled 'War, Peace and Peoples', where the bulk of the papers in this volume were first presented.

A version of Volker Berghahn's paper was subsequently published by Droste Verlag in *Marine und Marinepolitik, 1871-1914*, Dusseldorf, 1972. We are grateful for their permission to publish it in this collection.

INTRODUCTION

In an age when books made up of collections of essays are perhaps commoner than ever before and, on account of their frequent lack of unity and coherence, under fire as never before, the editors recognise an obligation to state at the outset their collection's theme and purpose. The purpose is precise enough. It posits the existence of a probably large body of serious-minded readers (whether professional scholars or not is of no matter) whose interest in war and society questions — that is in war and peace and the fates of peoples — exists outside or runs beyond the confines of the conventional academic disciplines and departments within which most professional scholars have to operate. Such people are not averse to mixed reading. Systematic, perhaps, in their reading of books and periodicals within the bounds of their accredited speciality or specialities, they like, so to speak, to do some reading ('meet people', 'pick up ideas') outside office hours. For such, the mixed conference, the anthology, the collection of essays are well suited. By the side of planned, systematic study, it is a somewhat haphazard approach to the higher sorts of learning, and some exact specialists find it too messy for comfort; but it seems to answer a good many respectable needs and, in the experience of some, to bring new lights and colours into work which might otherwise lack them.

Thus, in brief, runs the first part of the editors' statement of the book's purposes. The other two parts are unexceptionally orthodox and may be rapidly stated. These essays may be keeping mixed company between these covers, but none of them would look out of place in a periodical of conventional cut, and it is to be expected that many people will apply themselves to one or two of the essays without bothering themselves about the rest. That might be rather a pity — for these essays considerably inter-relate with each other, within their two groups. Finally, all these essays share the grand common purpose of all the social sciences: offering explanations for what has so far been inexplicable; releasing historical truths from prisons of pretentious ignorance, superstitious assertion, or self-interested duplicity; establishing patterns (admittedly provisional) of human and social behaviour where none yet are, or substituting more plausible patterns for others no longer credible; rationalising, clarifying and above all demythologising. In some such terms must the common purpose of social scientists and, so far as they are different, historians, be described. Ours in this book are no different — except that our eight essays are all to do with war and peace, and the myths which stand in our paths tend to pick up unusual power from their association with blood and death and ideas of honour, pride, manliness, race and nationality.

PART I

In the period from the fall of Napoleonic imperialism to the outbreak of the First World War armies and navies grew in complexity, cost and size. The first half of this book investigates these institutions from within, and looks at some of the factors which held them together in an increasingly difficult and hostile world, at their self-image, and at the pressures upon them from society at large. John Keegan points to the elements of continuity, to the sense of active history which pervades an army like the British which has a regimental structure as its base. Richard Luckett discusses the views which soldiers had of themselves and their performance as writers and critics of military life, views which differ markedly from those of critics looking from outside. Douglas Porch shows how one type of external pressure, republican ideology, was less effective at creating unrest within an army than the traditional discontents of military life; he suggests that the traditional categories by which we analyse armies need to be revised. Andrew Wheatcroft also reflects on the comparative weight of internal and external factors in determining an army's attitude, and concludes that 'professional' issues are those which truly divide armies from within. All these studies tend towards the common conclusion that we should no longer seek to apply the values of external society, but look instead for the values and attitudes which differentiate military society.

1 REGIMENTAL IDEOLOGY

John Keegan

This is an essay in amateur sociology, which sets out to answer a question probably only an amateur sociologist would ask: do national armies have individual 'characters' and, if so, what determines them? More precisely, it states and attempts to prove a hypothesis: that the British army's strong and distinctive character is the product, in large measure, of its unique internal structure; that the salient features of that structure are, nevertheless, and despite appearances to the contrary, common to many institutions of the English professional class; that the notable political docility of the British army is a function in part of the identity of outlook between soldier and civilian which those common features breed, but in part also a function of the peculiarity of the structure of the army itself; and, finally, but much more tentatively, that the 'anthropological' approach to the study of armies, which is the one through which this writer has achieved whatever perception he may have of the British army's character, is potentially of wider application, and is likely to prove, in our present state of ignorance about what armies are really like, a good deal more revealing than a conventionally sociological one.

But I must begin by disclaiming any credit for my adoption of the 'anthropological' approach, or for the resulting insights which it has offered me, for the truth is that I stumbled into it accidentally and by a roundabout route. I was, at the outset, merely trying to find my bearings in new and quite unfamiliar surroundings – those of the Royal Military Academy, Sandhurst, which I had joined, as a junior lecturer in military history, almost straight from Oxford. I knew, at the time, a little military history but nothing about the army or about how its officers were trained. 'What is Sandhurst?', was the question I therefore asked myself. Was it a sort of military university, like West Point, where academic achievement carried as much, if not more, weight than military performance? Or, like St-Cyr, was it a sort of novitiate, to which postulant officers came to try out their vocations and to be initiated into the rule of the order? Or was it a sort of super public school (where, as the local wits had it, 'the OTC had got out of hand')? That seemed the most likely analogy, not only because the public school is such a dominant institution-type in this country, and because of the well known and well documented link between the public schools and the army, but more simply because the Sandhurst Charter, I discovered, laid down specific aims for the Academy which, military allusions apart, might have been written by a great Victorian headmaster. They were, 'to develop in the officer cadet the essential characteristics of leadership, discipline and duty; to develop his physical fitness; and to lay the foundations of military and academic knowledge upon which the officer's future studies can be built'.[1]

After perhaps a year (I had joined the Academy in 1960), it began to dawn on me, however, that between the letter of the Charter and the spirit of Sandhurst life there yawned a divide. It was not that the staff or students sought to evade the Charter's prescriptions. On the contrary: military training was carried on with great energy and imagination and those parts of it which engaged the cadets' sense of adventure — overseas exercises, helicopter drill, field firing — were entered into with real enthusiasm. The academic courses were transmitted in a genuinely academic way and usually succeeded in generating a lively intellectual response. Games were played to a high competitive standard, and semi-vocational activities like sailing, gliding, flying, mountaineering and skindiving, which Sandhurst offered in a variety and at a cheapness which would make the average undergraduate blink with envy, had a strong following. Yet despite their ostentatious pursuit of the Academy's stated aims, and despite the recognised weight which professional perfection, academic achievement and athletic distinction carried in the assessment of an individual cadet's placing in the Order of Merit, I eventually came to conclude that staff and students were reserving their real energies for a different and quite private competition, of which the Academy officially knew almost nothing; that the object of that competition was the filling of regimental vacancies; and that Sandhurst was therefore neither university, nor seminary, nor public school, but some different sort of institution altogether which I was unable, and have subsequently ceased trying, to categorise.

Here must be described the method by which cadets and regiments choose each other. The match does not depend upon a cadet's position in the Order of Merit, though a high placing may improve his chance of securing or even bettering his first choice of regiment, and a low placing may jeopardise the promise of a regimental vacancy already given. These caveats aside, it would be true to say that the parties concerned — the cadet on the one hand, the regiment on the other — strike their bargain direct, either before the young man joins Sandhurst (the Greenjackets have a particularly extensive network of talent scouts among the staff of the leading public schools) or through the regimental representative during the cadet's time at the Academy. The regimental representative can make only a tentative offer; it is confirmed after the candidate has been interviewed by a panel of the regiment's senior officers, who will normally include a number of serving or retired generals. Sandhurst intervenes in this process only to the extent of allocating the total of available vacancies between the regiments and recording the names of those who eventually fill them — a quite different procedure from that, say, at St-Cyr, where the cadet first in the Order of Merit has first pick of the vacancies, and so on downwards. The Academy does, of course, prescribe after proper consultation certain minimum entrance standards to the different regiments and corps; but as these apply stringently only to the less combatant — and therefore less popular — branches, the main bargaining process is scarcely affected. That process I came to compare, fairly early in my acquaintance with Sandhurst, to a marriage market; and it was the same analogy which struck an American sociology student who was given permission to do his doctoral work at the Academy in 1968.[2] What separately alerted us to the crucial importance of pair-bonding between regiments and cadets was not, at least in my case, the deployment of any unusual power of perception or of an informed sociological sense. It was a simple observation of what seemed most to exercise cadets and instructors (who are also the regimental representatives), measured in terms of their own assessment of their 'success' or 'failure'. For just as cadets want to be accepted by the 'best' regiment which they have a realistic chance of joining, so instructors are anxious to secure the 'best' cadets for the vacancies they have to fill. To this preoccupation, almost everything else at Sandhurst is secondary.

But merely to have observed the importance attached to regimental selection was not, of course, to have explained it. So how to explain it? One can begin by showing that a Hobson's choice of regiment (and some cadets are necessarily left with Hobson's choice) will limit both vertically and laterally the broad pattern of an officer's career from the outset. Entry into the technical Corps, for example, means that an officer's range of activity is going to be confined fairly strictly to the technical functions which his Corps performs, and that he can expect promotion only within its own hierarchy. The officer who joins the Royal Electrical and Mechanical Engineers, the Royal Army Ordnance Corp, Royal Corps of Transport, or even the Royal Signals, which between them recruit almost a third of all officer entrants, cannot therefore look forward to becoming a senior general staff officer; he has a much reduced chance of entry to the Staff College, the gateway to a generalist career in the Army; and he will spend most of his service either supervising workshops, controlling transport or caretaking stores. No wonder that a lively and ambitious young man, unless he has a genuinely technical bent, should look automatically to the regiments of cavalry, artillery and infantry (though also to the Corps of Royal Engineers which, for historical reasons counts as a combatant regiment),[3] since that way lies variety, promotion and, by extension, prestige.

But that does not explain the importance attached by an individual cadet to securing acceptance by a particular regiment, nor why he should prefer one regiment over another. An immediate guess might be that some regiments offer better promotion prospects than others, in the same way that all regiments do over all corps. But that is not so. It is true that the High Command in the First World War is often loosely categorised as a collection of 'cavalry generals', and that Haig, Byng and Gough, to name the Commander-in-Chief and two of his Army Commanders in France *were* cavalrymen. But of the others, Horne was a gunner, Plumer from the York and Lancaster Regiment, Rawlinson a Rifleman, and Birdwood originally a Royal Scots Fusilier. Moreover, of the Second World War generals, though Gort, now in process of rehabilitation, and Alexander were Guardsmen, Montgomery was a County Infantryman (a Warwick), Wavell a Highlander (Black Watch), and Auchinleck and Slim from the Indian Army, socially the poor relation of the British. Promotion beyond the regiment, in short, is generally by merit, promotion to the top exclusively by merit as, I would venture to argue, it has been throughout the last hundred years; and I do not think it possible to show even a random connection between the attainment of high rank in the British army and particular regimental origins, as it is in the old German army, if the curious case of the third Garde-Regiment zu Fuss means anything.[4]

Why then the attraction between an individual cadet and a particular regiment? It might be explained in terms of social competitiveness, for as is well known, British regiments may be arranged in a sort of pecking order, well drawn by Simon Raven in his *Encounter* essay, 'Perish by the Sword'.[5] The Foot Guards, Household Cavalry, four or five regiments of Cavalry of the Line, and the Greenjackets would be put at the top, the rest of the Cavalry next, slightly below them the Highland regiments (though coequal, if not superior, by their own reckoning), then the Light Infantry and Fusiliers, following those the Southern English County and Lowland Scots regiments, and last the Irish, Welsh, Northern and Midland regiments. Somewhere in the middle would come the Royal Artillery and Royal Engineers, which demand special professional attainments, and the Royal Tank and Parachute Regiments, which cultivate a rather bogus specialist outlook. But to imply, as a theory of naked competitiveness would demand, that all cadets make a bid for the top and then, as in a Dutch auction, drop back until they can find a taker, would be to misrepresent events. The English social system is not as *arriviste* as that and the Sandhurst social climber who misses a rung gets short shrift on the way down. It would be unkind to indicate exactly where he is likely to end up, but safe to say that regiments which would have responded warmly to his overtures in the first instance will very often spurn him once he has been refused elsewhere.

This should not, in my view, be seen as evidence of regimental pique, the wounded reaction of the thin-skinned. It suggests to me, on the contrary, that most regiments have a very robust sense of identity, are looking for a cadet whose identity tallies with their their own — since they are stuck with him for life once they take him on — and have little patience to spend on the trimmer or the wobbler. The average cadet, who knows for his part that what each regiment has to offer is its own particular way of life and circle of friendship, is usually quick to grasp the point, and to make up his own mind about what sort of person he is (or can successfully pass himself off as being).

What, in short, we are dealing with is a question of image, perceived image but, more important, also self-image, and the first question about it to settle — since regimental self-image is crucial to an understanding of the British army's character and behaviour — is that of how it was formed. In the case of the regiments at the top of Mr Raven's pecking order — Guards, Greenjackets, Cavalry, Highlanders — formation took place at an early date and has a fairly obvious root cause. The Guards' derives from their constant proximity to the sovereign, the Cavalry's from the afterglow of Chivalry, the Greenjackets' from the romance of their Peninsula achievements, the Highlanders' from their semi-savage origins and now grossly exaggerated tribal character. But the self-image of the more numerous, workaday County regiments is of much more recent formation and to examine when and how it took shape one must return to the era of the Cardwell and post-Cardwell reforms of the 1870s and 1880s.

The nature of these reforms will be familiar. They entailed the substitution of short- for long-service enlistment of private soldiers, the abolition of the purchase of commissions by officers, the pairing of single into double battalion regiments and their 'localisation' in permanent recruiting areas. It is therefore from Cardwell (though to be precise from 1881, when he had already ceased to be Secretary of War), that the County Regiment dates, and that is true even though some regiments had borne County titles since the 1750s. What ensured the new regiments' assumption of a genuinely County character, which the earlier allocation of titles had not done, was the location of each regimental depot in the region from which it was supposed to recruit (even though many regiments continued to make good deficiencies with Irishmen and Londoners); and the affiliation to the regiment of the local Militia and Volunteer battalions, the citizen soldiers of the area.

Now the principal effect intended by these reforms was to provide more economically and efficiently for the garrisoning of the Empire. In that intention, as Brian Bond has shown, Cardwell's reforms only partially succeeded.[6] But it was also an intention of his to transform the basis on which the army was officered, the means he chose being the abolition of the property qualification (i.e. purchase). Here one must quickly forestall the objection that abolition was a precondition for the whole package, an objective whose force must, of course, be accepted. But what surely can be said in this respect is that Cardwell — and by no means only Cardwell — was also anxious to attract officer candidates from the rising middle classes. The bait he offered was 'entry by competition' and 'promotion by merit', a promise — or a threat — nicely calculated both to attract the energetic 'new man' and to frighten the worst of the merely monied among serving officers into a show of military zeal.

In this respect, again, his intentions were not wholly to be realised. It has been one of the strongest arguments of the defenders of purchase that the system preserved the independence of the officers and the peace of the realm by obstructing favouritism — favouritism being seen as a means by which an overmighty subject might make the army his creature and use it to overturn the established order. Whatever the realities of that danger, they were very effectively brought into play during the abolition period, for the army managed to represent promotion by merit (though *not* entry by open competition) as equivalent to favouritism. As a result it secured the institution of a system of promotion by *seniority* 'tempered by the threat of suspension for incompetence'. The cause of progress, it may therefore be thought, was only doubtfully served by this particular outcome of the reform programme.

If the reader has been led to that conclusion, he way well have been led astray. For it is my contention, on the contrary, that the 1870s and 1880s did see the emergence of a 'new' officer, but an officer not so much of a new *class* as of a new *sort*; a man who was in part the product of the Cardwell *aggiorniamento* but also of a movement in British society of which the Cardwell reforms were themselves an effect. For Cardwell was of course not, as I implied earlier, confronted by any difficulty in attracting officer recruits from the new middle class. Quite the opposite was true; that class was hammering at the doors of the army, as it had hammered at and broken down those of the Indian Civil Service (1853), the Home Civil Service and — a partial break-in — the Royal Military Academy, Woolwich (1863) — the dates are those when competition replaced nomination as the method of entry. This assault on privilege can be represented in simple economic terms as a search for *lebensraum*, an effort by the new and greatly enlarged middle class to obtain for its sons a fairer share of those scarce, secure salaried positions hitherto monopolised by the propertied. But it is unlikely, certainly in the case of purchase, that the new men would have pushed as hard, nor the old yielded as easily, had the sons in question not already learnt, or more precisely been taught, the code of manners and set of assumptions which the Victorian gentleman would have expected to find in a brother officer. The campaign, in short, could not have been won had the ground not been prepared by the reformed public schools; certainly those who reaped its fruits were almost exclusively public school boys.

In no sense, however, was the boy from the reformed public school a new boy to the army. By 1870, the Arnoldian schools had, to borrow a term from the oil industry, come fully 'on stream', had indeed been supplying the army with their products for the last twenty years. One of the new schools — Wellington — had been founded in 1841 as an English counterpart to the Prytanee,[7] and others, notably Cheltenham (1841), Marlborough (1843) and Clifton (1862), had quickly established a strong army connection. Certainly by 1885, Sandhurst, by then virtually the only route into the Infantry and Cavalry, was filled as to 85 per cent with boys from public schools, either from the new foundations or from older ones which had been reformed, notably Eton, Harrow, Winchester, Charterhouse and Sherborne. We may take it, therefore, that there can have been little friction on first acquaintance between the pre- and post-purchase officers, for though the proportion of new middle class entrants rose quite sharply at Sandhurst between 1870 and 1890, from about 10 per cent to about 37 per cent, they would probably have been difficult to distinguish outwardly from entrants from the traditional sectors (of which army families had always been the largest). Both sorts of entrant, indeed, might well have been at school together beforehand.

Public school was a perfect preparation for a military career, an observation none the less true for being hackneyed. For late nineteenth-century public schools inculcated many of the military qualities — physical fitness, skill at games, toughness, love of the outdoors — and taught most of the military virtues — obedience, companionability, leadership, concern for the welfare of subordinates. The post-purchase public school officer, whether from a new or a traditional army family, was therefore likely to join his regiment a far more finished product than the old-fashioned purchase officer. But, more important, he was joining an institution which not only insisted on his possession of those qualities and virtues but which, in its post-Cardwell transformation, was itself to become a school of perfection, able on the one hand to refuse entry to candidates whom it found deficient, on the other to require of its members increasingly high standards of concern for the soldiers' welfare, personal self-sacrifice, social conformity and military efficiency.

How did this come about? In the first place, because the Cardwell system had, quite accidentally, made loyalty *to* the regiment and service *within* the regiment, and to no other regiment, the passport to a successful career. Under purchase, an officer had got on by buying the steps up to his lieutenant-colonelcy as quickly as possible, since the younger he was when he got to that rank the better his chance of becoming a general. To get it he might transfer half a dozen times in twenty years. The Commission on Purchase, examining the records of 52 of the most distinguished general officers, found that while 12 had served always in one regiment, 4 had served in two, 8 in three, 9 in four, 11 in five, 4 in six, 3 in seven, and 1 in nine.[8] The unfavourable effect that this sort of gadfly careerism exerted on regimental efficiency and on the poorer officers' morale had long been a cause of scandal. The Cardwell system extinguished it, for the principle of offering promotion by seniority *within the regiment* (which had not been abolished with purchase) had the effect of keeping the lieutenant-colonelcy in the regiment's hands; while the new threat of passing-over for incompetence (which in practice could also mean slackness or insufferability) encouraged among officers a spirit of cooperation and of decently unostentatious zeal, since their futures now hung not upon raising the price of a step but on the contents of their confidential reports and the results of their promotion exams.

But to imply that the late Victorian or Edwardian officer became, through the abolition of purchase, a mere paper chaser would be altogether to misrepresent his approach to regimental life. It was far more positive and far more warm blooded than that. Indeed I do not feel it exaggerated to say that from 1870 onwards one witnesses the beginning of something if not like a live affair then certainly like a protracted infatuation between the British officer and his regiment. Nor should that surprise us. For the regiment embodied half a dozen features of the strongest appeal to the upper middle class Victorian, by which we also mean the Arnoldian public school boy. The following are the most obvious ones:

Ancient lineage: most of the regiments were of respectable age and the senior twenty-five had been raised before James II's deposition.
Landed interest: Cardwell's 'localisation' scheme had implanted the regiment in county life and, in doing so, conferred county status on its officers – for those not born to it, an extremely gratifying privilege.
Connections at Court: many of the regiments had members of the Royal Family as Honorary Colonels, which conferred a gratifying sense of communion with the great.
Self-government: command of the regiment, as we have seen had become virtually elective and admission to the regiment had entered into its gift; these two factors combined to make it almost as completely a self-governing corporation as those against which the rising middle class had battered so hard during the last days of patronage.

To these factors we must add the attractions of a mess life little different from that of the best London clubs, of almost unfettered opportunity to play and to organise any sort of game and sport, of a strong but satisfying obligation to oversee the physical welfare of the deserving poor in the persons of their soldiers and their families, and in addition, the duty — welcomed by many officers — of setting them an inspiring example of Christian leadership. One of the campaigns which Arnold had waged most enthusiastically was to obtain ecclesiastical authority for the administration of Holy Communion to soldiers by their officers, when a priest was not to be had. It had failed — to many officers' regret, one suspects.

This profile of the regiment I have drawn is probably reminiscent of that of other major British institutions, salient features, for example, of the Oxford and Cambridge college system and of the Inns of Court being the intermingling of the social and business sides of everyday life, the practice of commensality, the exercise of a jealously guarded autonomy and the profession, spoken or unspoken, of a belief that the institution should pursue some larger end than its functional purpose prescribes. But the institution of which the Cardwell regiment even more vividly reminds me is that of the large, comfortable Victorian county family, from which some of the officers came and to which the rest would have liked to belong. One is reminded of it by the way in which regiments began to collect ornamental and commemorative silver in enormous quantities (little regimental silver antedates 1850), to commission histories and presentation protraits, to buy pictures and furniture, to decorate regimental chapels in the local cathedral or county town church and fill them with funerary monuments, to build cottages for regimental pensioners, to set up regimental charities and trust funds, to organise regimental 'cricket weeks', to endow handicap events at local race meetings, even to buy regimental horses and yachts. Inevitably, too, they fostered marriages, thus ensuring a supply of future officers bred in their ways.

These families were successful families. They extended their circle of kinship, friendship and acquaintance into the civil society which surrounded them, not only at the social level of the officers but down to the grassroots. It is this implantation of the British Infantry regiment into regional life which helps, I am sure, to explain the nation's success, twice in this century, in building up giant citizen armies on the sketchiest of regular frameworks. The volunteers who flocked foward in 1914 and 1915, and their conscript sons of 1939, went off not to be 'eaten by the *Gare de l'Est*',[9] not to disappear inside a faceless juggernaut, but to join an identifiable unit whose reputation was part of local folklore, whose Territorials were a familiar and slightly comic part of the local scene and whose infinitely expandable structure offered accommodation to as many battalions as the resident population could raise. The citizen battalions of 1914-15, in particular, drew enormous strength from their assumption of the name, tradition and fighting records of their regular parent regiments — and needed to, since they lacked any adequate cadre of trained officers and NCOs.

Today the regiments, because of successive cuts in the size of the army, have diminished in number. But the manner in which they have responded to the imposition of the cuts bears out, if anything, the family analogy. Only two or three have accepted extinction. Many others, under compulsion, have amalgamated, two by two or three by three, usually with county neighbours, sometimes with a more distant but more compatible *esprit*. And in one or two fascinating cases, notably that of the Light Infantry regiments, there has taken place what one might call a 'consolidation of holdings', in anticipation of cuts threatened but not yet imposed. The four Light Infantry regiments — Durham, Shropshire, Yorkshire, Somerset and Cornwall — sensing the empending reduction of one of their number, hastily arranged a merger which has preserved the existence of all at the expense of some blurring of their identities. It is this ability and willingness to adapt, to accept the necessity for larger groupings, now also facing the administrative counties, the local police authorities and countless other British institutions, which convinces one that the British regimental system is still alive and kicking. But its willingness to give ground should not be taken as implying a readiness to be stampeded. Neither officers nor men give any sign of being prepared to be parcelled up together in that cost-effective monstrosity, a Corps of Infantry; and the success of the cavalry regiments in resisting the development of the Royal Armoured Corps, into which they were all incorporated in 1939, into an effective supraregimental authority suggests that the organisers of a Corps of Infantry would have a tooth-and-nail struggle to make it work. Whitehall's and Westminster's enthusiasm for regimental rationalisation has, in any case, been much diminished by the 'Save the Argylls' campaign of 1969-71, which resulted in the delivery to Downing Street of the largest collection of signatures ever appended to a petition in British political history.

But what importance, all in all, does the survival of the historic British regiments hold, except for antiquarians? The antiquarian interest is strong enough in itself, for the senior regiments are now some of the oldest corporate institutions in Europe, outranking, for example, the Academie Française, the Bank of England, and many time encrusted Oxford and Cambridge colleges, and rivalling in age the Society of Jesus and the Hudson's Bay Company. Indeed, were some of the regiments not fighting units but buildings — Victorian railway stations, say, or Jacobean almshouses — the probability is that Sir John Betjeman would have sprung forward to protest at the first threat to the continued existence of any one of them; it is yet not impossible to envisage him demanding the making of a ministerial preservation order, say, on the Royal Welsh Fusiliers, now approaching its three-hundredth birthday and bearing on its colours mementoes of the battles of the Boyne, Blenheim, Bunker's Hill, Badajoz, Waterloo, Inkerman, Lucknow and the defence of the Peking Legations.

However risible civilians might find such a notion, moreover, soldiers at least would see the point. For armies, besides being intensely conservative institutions, have long recognised, well before it was discovered by social psychologists, that effective human groups are subject to laws of scale; that the group of regimental size, about 600 to 1,000 strong, has a particular tactical value; and that its value is enhanced by stability and its by-products: reputation, corporate self-image, tradition — especially traditions of loyalty and courage. Unique though British military institutions may be in their antiquity, other armies accord them the flattery of imitation. Modern French regiments, almost none of which can trace an unbroken lineage beyond 1944, all wear on their uniforms the insignia of their putative ancestors in the army of the *ancien régime*. The American army, in its post-Korean reconstruction, adopted a Combat Arms Regimental System (CARS) in a not altogether successful attempt to foster Revolutionary and Civil War parents on to the unregistered offspring of the Second World War. And in the Bundeswehr, which is virtually a forbidden memory by constitutional edict, regiments nevertheless constantly seek to establish themselves as the authentic *Traditionsträger* of vanished units of the Kaiser's.

Mere antiquity is not, however, the reason why the British regimental system deserves serious attention. Within its national context, it has a much more general importance. For the British army is, as we know, the only major European army which has no recent record of intervention in politics, none, indeed, excepting the Curragh incident, since the seventeenth century. Now, the quick and easy explaining away of what Holmes would have called this 'curious incident of the dog in the night-time'[10] is that the British army has had no occasion or motive to intervene in politics;[11] the British have had no Petain because they have suffered no *Débacle*, have known no *Freikorps* because they have been spared a *Zusammenbruch*. And that is true and valid, of course. Motive and occasion have a habit, however, of presenting themselves for inspection only after parade is over; and it is my contention that if the British army and the state have avoided a parade ground confrontation during the last hundred years, the regimental system has been instrumental in averting it.

Take first the question of motive, or disposition. The officers of the purchase army were reckoned individually indisposed to play politics because the capital they had tied up in commissions was a token of indemnity — 'caution money', which would go forfeit for bad behaviour. Collectively, as an important *rentier* group, their interest lay, in any case, in preserving the order of things as they knew them. But with the abolition of purchase, the interest of the group was potentially liable to change. Any government, anywhere, any time, even at a time and place as stable as late Victorian England, is running a risk when it changes the basis of its contract with its officers, and the risk which Cardwell and Gladstone ran, or, rather, bequeathed to their successors, was of transforming the body of British officers into an officer corps. That the officers, no longer independent investors, but salaried — and poorly salaried — employees, failed to develop any sense of common 'officership', of membership of an all-army corporation with its own legitimate interests, we may reasonably ascribe to the success of the Cardwell regiments in totally capturing their loyalties (in a way I like to think analogous to Konrad Lorenz's capture of baby ducklings through the process he calls 'imprinting').

Over the matter of 'occasion to intervene' we can be much less tentative. Those who hold that recent British history has presented the army with no issue over which it might strike political attitudes quite ignore the fact that its primary role, during the last one hundred and seventy years, has been the defence of an empire, most of which it itself won in battle. While the Empire grew, while it merely flourished, the politics of Empire were a matter which the army might quite readily have been expected to leave to Parliament, if only because its energies were fully and rewardingly occupied in imperial activity. Once the Empire began to diminish, however, and particularly once the orderly disengagement of British authority from the Empire became a duty which fell foursquare on the army, the likelihood might well have been that it began to kick. Such, certainly, was the experience of the Fourth Republic, whose soldiers so conducted the war in Indo-China that it culminated in the greatest possible humiliation of the French Far Eastern presence, and subsequently, during the Algerian war, mounted a *putsch* whenever they suspected the government of slackening its will to win.

Most of the indiscipline manifested by the French army was the work of a minority, of units of the Armée d'Afrique and the Armée coloniale, the two forces with which France garrisoned and policed her empire. And their efforts were frustrated, when they were, not so much by the loyalty as by the bloody-mindedness of the conscripts of the Armée métropolitaine, who were damned if they were going to support any move which threatened to prolong the war and hence their term of service. What this episode tells us is how thankful we should be that Britain always forebore to create a large white Colonial Army, with interests and prestige invested in the preservation of the Empire. Our escape was perhaps a narrow one, for if Arnold-Forster, the Conservative Secretary for War, 1904-6, had had his way, he would have brought just such a body into being. What deterred him from doing so was the anticipated resistance of the existing regiments to a scheme which would have entailed the disbandment of some thirty of their number.

Our Empire continued to be garrisoned, therefore, by the Cardwell regiments which, when his scheme worked properly, always had one of its battalions at home to feed the other abroad. Abroad might be Egypt, Malta, Austria, China, though most often India but, in so far as the exact location was concerned. it mattered little to the life or spirit of the regiment itself. None ever looked like putting down roots, for its roots lay in its home recruiting area, while it drew its sustenance from its own resources, and most copiously from its sense of difference from others. There I think, lies the explanation of the army's strange but admirable composure during the painful and difficult withdrawal from the Far East, from East Africa, from Cyprus, from Arabia and the Persian Gulf. 'Exactly what I would have expected of the Argylls. Never really knew how to carry out orders', are the sort of words you might have heard from a Northumberland Fusilier in Aden in 1967 after Mad Mitch's Nelsonian reoccupation of Crater. While regiments feel this about each other, hug their sense of difference tight about themselves, cultivate separatism and are prepared to recall days when they did not belong to the British army at all — the Royal Scots was first in Swedish, then in French service, the Queen's Regiment originally in Dutch — there seems to be little prospect of any two of them making common cause against anyone but the Queen's enemies. As Michael Howard put it in an *Encounter* article in 1962,[12] 'The regimental system may isolate the military but it also tames them, fixing their eyes on minutiae, limiting their ambitions, teaching them a gentle, parochial loyalty difficult to pervert to more dangerous ends.'

This sense of regimental difference, to give a concrete example of its strength and pervasiveness, has recently tightened its grip even at Sandhurst where, in fulfilment of a new scheme of officer training, the students have, since March 1973, been commissioned as probationary second lieutenants after six months and now complete their regular officer training clad in all the variety of their regimental uniforms. This new scheme is in itself an admission of the strength of the regimental system, for, at a time of shortage in officer recruiting, many regiments had taken to persuading applicants to go to the short service officer school at Mons Barracks, thus reducing, for the cadet, the time spent in training from two years to five months and, for the regiment, averting the danger of its prize being poached during the more leisurely period of regimental selection at Sandhurst. The army, apparently able to think of no other way of ending this free-for-all, closed Mons — but reduced the precommissioning period at Sandhurst by nineteen months. The result is that, though all regiments get an equal crack at the cadets and *vice versa*, the shortening of the time available for the marriage market to operate has even further served to enhance its importance within the Sandhurst system.

Michael Lewis, surveying the rise of the modern naval officer, which he represents in terms of a struggle between the ship captains, wishing to take as cadets whomsoever they chose, and the Admiralty, insistent upon minimum standards of competence, records[13] that in 1870, on the implementation of Limited Competition, 'the Admiralty, not the Captains, at long last had the choice of the next generation of naval officers . . . At long last [it] ruled its own house.' One wonders if today, a hundred years after Cardwell abolished purchase, we can pass the same verdict on relations between the Army Board and the regiments.

This brief and impressionistic account of what one observer has seen of the day-to-day workings of a single army is inevitably a partial and distorted one. I remain convinced that the regiment is, nevertheless, the most significant of Britain's military institutions, the principal vehicle of the nation's military culture, if one may so describe it, and a factor by no means without significance in the country's political and social history. It is possible, however, that that importance has now just begun to drain away from the regiments and move towards the staff colleges and schools, through which in future all officers, not merely the able and ambitious, will make their careers. If that were to be so, it would be very much in accordance with Professor Huntington's theory that 'professionalism' must become the ethic of a genuine democracy's army.[14] My own suspicion, however, is that both he and Professor Janowitz,[15] who foresees the transformation of the American army into a body almost of a civil service character, are advancing judgements which, though perfectly relevant to the army they know at first hand, are very doubtfully applicable to others, least of all to Britain's. For the concept of 'heroic' leadership, of which both, as good citizens of the republic, are understandably suspicious, is not one which strikes the same *frisson* of alarm here as there. We want and expect our soldiers to be 'heroic'; whether, indeed, armies can function effectively in the absence of an 'heroic' example, many would doubt. My own observation is that the only currency of unchallengeable value which circulates in an army is a reputation for courage; that that reputation can scarcely be earned outside a fighting regiment; that neither 'professionalism' nor civil service values commonly flourish there; and that military leaders, at least on this side of the Atlantic, will continue therefore to cultivate an 'heroic' style. As it happens, the British regiment provides a perfect, self-enclosed forum wherein 'heroic' leadership can operate.

It also offers one of the most fascinating objects of study still unexplored in an advanced industrial society. But a note of caution: regiments cannot be taken unawares or by storm. Their private world is a silent, often secretive one. They close ranks automatically against uninvited intruders, and are expert at concealing their business from outside authority. But the student who is prepared to seek an introduction, to listen, to watch, to make friends, above all to wait, is likely to find his tact and patience amply and warmly rewarded.

Notes

1.   Since its radical reorganisation in the spring of 1973, Sandhurst has had a differently worded charter. Its sense remains, however, broadly as before.
2.   Maurice Garnier, 'Social class and military socialisation', unpublished Ph.D. thesis, University of California, 1972. A copy is lodged in the Central Library, RMA Sandhurst.
3.   The Royal Engineers is, by nearly two centuries, the oldest of the corps, to which it has progressively shed its more technical (e.g. electrical and mechanical repair) functions as they have been brought into being. The main role it preserves is that of 'combat engineering' – bridge laying and road making in the face of the enemy. From that derives its cherished 'teeth arm' status.
4.   The Kaiser's Third Foot Guards was the regiment into which Hindenburg was commissioned in 1870. His son Oskar and the future generals or field-marshals Schleicher (Chancellor, 1932), Hammerstein-Equord (Commander-in-Chief, 1932-4), Brauchitsch (Commander-in-Chief, 1938-41), and Manstein (Commander, Army Group South, 1942-3) all followed him into the regiment, just before or after the turn of the century.
5.   Simon Raven, 'Perish by the sword', reprinted in *The Establishment*, ed. Hugh Thomas, Blond, 1959.
6.   See Brian Bond's series of articles in the *Royal United Service Institution Journal*, 1960, pp. 213 ff, 1961, pp. 229 ff.
7.   The Prytanée de la Flèche was founded by Napoleon to provide free education of a military character for the sons of dead, wounded or otherwise deserving officers. Many of its pupils ('les Brutieux') have always gone on to St-Cyr.
8.   Sir Robert Biddulph, *Lord Cardwell at the War Office*, John Murray, 1904.
9.   The Gare de l'Est is the Paris terminus from which the Fifth Military Region's reservists left for the frontier in 1914. 'Mangé par le Gare de l'Est' became a fashionable pacifist expression in the inter-war period.
10.   Sir Arthur Conan Doyle, 'Silver Blaze' in *The Memoirs of Sherlock Holmes*, George Newnes, 1893.

> 'Is there anything to which you would wish to draw my attention?'
> 'To the curious incident of the dog in the night-time.'
> 'The dog did nothing in the night-time.'
> 'That was the curious incident', remarked Sherlock Holmes.

11.   'Disposition' and 'opportunity' are the two correlates on which Professor S. E. Finer bases his theory of the 'Role of the Military in Politics'. See *The Man*

on Horseback, Pall Mall Press, 1962.
12. Michael Howard, 'Soldiers in politics', *Encounter*, No. 108, September 1962, pp. 77-81.
13. Michael Lewis, *The Navy in Transition*, Hodder and Stoughton, 1965, p. 109.
14. See Samuel P. Huntington, *The Soldier and the State*, Harvard University Press, 1959, *passim*.
15. Morris Janowitz, *The Professional Soldier*, Free Press, 1960.

2 PRE-REVOLUTIONARY ARMY LIFE IN RUSSIAN LITERATURE

Richard Luckett

When Harold Wilson rhetorically demanded, in the course of the 1964 election camapign, 'Why do I say so much about the Royal Navy?', a voice from the crowd replied, with sufficient appositeness, 'Because you're in Chatham.' If we ask why so many Russian writers of the pre-revolutionary period dealt at some length with the military life we are inviting a similar reply: because they lived in Russia. There were, of course, other reasons besides; at the beginning of his story 'The Raid' (1852) Tolstoy's narrator tells us that:

> 'War always interests me: not war in the sense of manoeuvres devised by great generals — my imagination refused to follow such immense movements, I did not understand them — but the reality of war, the actual killing. I was more interested to know in what way and under the influence of what feeling one soldier kills another than to know how the armies were arranged at Austerlitz and Borodino.'[1]

The passage contains ironies enough, for Tolstoy, as distinct from his narrator, was to become fascinated by grand strategy (for all that he would eventually use his knowledge of it to endeavour to demonstrate its triviality) as well as by individual combat; in due course he was to write a novel which treats equally of both. In any case few of Tolstoy's readers, whether of his own time or the present, are likely to miss the personal note in his military writings; indeed, in *Sketches from Sevastopol* that the 'you' who by proxy conducts the reader into the beleaguered town was originally Tolstoy himself is an essential part of the total effect of the account, a guarantee of authenticity. Tolstoy was involved in military life; he was interested in it of necessity. He was involved because in the Russia of his time it had become the only alternative to a career in the ranks of the civil service or to stagnation in the provinces, cut off from the company of social and intellectual equals. For Tolstoy in April 1851 the tedium of Yasnaya Polyana led to an incontinence of which he fundamentally disapproved; it also led to gambling bouts, which he subsequently regretted as bitterly as he did his incontinence, and which he could less well afford. The solutions he proposed — systematic gambling, a career in the civil service, marriage to an heiress — were all, as his brother Nicholas pointed out, deeply unsatisfactory. At Nicholas's suggestion, therefore, Leo accompanied his brother to the Caucasus where, irritated by the disdain evinced by Nicholas's fellow officers in the garrison for the 'civilian', he persuaded Prince Baryatinsky, in command of the left wing of the Army of the Caucasus, to take him on as a volunteer. By December he had applied for a commission.[2]

The casual fashion in which this came about demonstrates how a man who was in most respects a totally unlikely candidate might find himself an officer. It is salutary to remember that Lermontov, Bakunin, Dostoevsky and Kuprin all served in the army, that Kurochkin, the editor of *Iskra*, did six years in the Dvoryansk regiment, and that Chernyshevsky was for a time a teacher in a military academy. Goncharov (the author of *Oblomov*) spent a period in the navy – which, from what we know of his character, seems almost inconceivable.[3] The army had even played a direct part in literary affairs in the eighteenth century, when it owned the only licensed printing presses in Russia; in a different way it influenced the literary history of the nineteenth century, since the gibes at *patriotistika* that circulated in cartoon and pamphlet form throughout the army after its defeat in the Crimean War played their part in the emergence of a popular satirical press.[4] The involvement of Russian writers with the military life was a function of experience, and this is a vital point. For it is a serious weakness in the case for making the so-called 'social novel' of the nineteenth century the basis of quasi-historical observations that the texts most widely considered were produced away from direct experience of the circumstances that they described. The novels written from experience lack those literary qualities that would ensure them sympathetic consideration – though it should hardly occasion surprise that the working classes were not the novel writing classes. So we substitute middle class accounts, written – with however much sympathy – at secondhand, and fail to note how radical this transposition is. Russian literature with a military setting is by no means free from the difficulty, but the teleological problem is certainly far less in evidence.

There are, however, some necessary qualifications which we must not ignore. Lermontov's *A Hero of Our Time* (1840) occupies a vital place not only in the genealogy of the Russian novel but also, I believe, in the genesis of a character-type fashionable in Russia through to the revolutionary period, and even beyond. This is, of course, the notion of the 'superfluous man'. Pechorin, the hero, can find no opening in Russian society that will adequately utilise his talents. He joins the army and, his malaise exacerbated by the military context – the tedium, the arbitrariness, the dubious rationale of violence – devotes himself to the destruction of whatever comes to hand, irrespective of whether it is a woman's spirit or another man's life. Naturally enough there have been critics who have seen this as an indictment of the Tsarist army in particular, and of Tsarist society in general. They have a pretty formidable case. But the sympathetic portrayal of Maxim Maximich, the doggedly 'professional' officer who plays an important part in the book as the foil to Pechorin, is a serious threat to their argument. Take Maxim Maximich seriously and Pechorin becomes largely an oddity — an oddity characteristic of 'Our Times', as the title suggests, but an oddity nevertheless. As an older school of criticism tells us, he is a variant of the Byronic hero, out of the same stable as Evgeny Onegin. Yet he is not merely a literary type; he comes alive because he has his equivalents in real life — indeed there are points at which he reminds us of Pushkin himself, who took part in the Caucasian campaign of 1829 as — so his most illuminating critic tells us — 'a poet, informal war correspondent, would-be lancer, *bon vivant*, and semi-professional gamester'.[5]

But Lermontov did not merely describe; he also created. He crystallised the characteristics of a type, and by doing so opened the way for a thousand imitations. In his preface Lermontov had complained that in Russia: 'Our reading public remains immature and does not understand allegory unless it finds a moral at the end. It cannot solve riddles nor appreciate irony; it is downright badly educated.' The accuracy of this observation was proven by the reception of his own book. Pechorins — or, rather, pale imitations — became two a penny. His attitudes (aristocratic *hauteur*, fearlessness, total cynicism, all of these things being consciously aimed for and achieved) were widely copied, and in the imitation became affectations of an affectation. The imitation turns up as an authentic and credible type in both Tolstoy and Dostoevsky, and in the documentary *Sketches from Sevastopol* one of the devices by which Tolstoy endeavours to shock his readers into an awareness of the realities of modern warfare is the portrayal of men who have adopted this façade but are unable, in times of extremity, to avoid letting it slip. Even in Kuprin's great novel of military life, *The Duel* (1905), there are still Pechorinesque characters, and the scrupulous realism of Kuprin's style brings home to us the fact that they are portrayals of real people, not derivatives of a literary model, except in so far as, between Lermontov and Kuprin, literature had become life.

The conflict between professionals and amateurs, already evident in *A Hero of Our Time*, is a basic theme in Russian military affairs and hence in the literature of army life; it might even be claimed that it was exacerbated by such literature. It will be noted that whilst, as in the case of Lermontov, this could always be seen as a criticism of the society that produced the amateurs, it could also be seen as an exhortation to be professional. But on the whole the point is not made in an hortatory way. This was not merely because of the insufficiently considered fact that, in Tsarist Russia, it was often safer to criticise destructively than to have the temerity to offer constructive advice. (That this was the case can be established from a glance at the censored and uncensored versions of Tolstoy's military tales.) The real reason was that the army was seen primarily as a way of life, and only secondarily as an institution that was subject to change in any positive way. This is itself as important a point as the amateurs versus professionals controversy. When in Book V of *War and Peace* Nicholas Rostov returns to his regiment he reflects that:

> 'Here in the regiment all was clear and simple. The whole world was divided into two unequal parts: one, our Pavlograd regiment; the other, all the rest. And the rest was no concern of his. In the regiment everything was definite: who was lieutenant, who captain, who was a good fellow, who a bad one, and most of all, who was a comrade . . . there was nothing to think about or decide, you had only to do nothing that was considered bad in the Pavlograd regiment and, when given an order, to do what was clearly, distinctly, and definitely ordered — and all would be well.'

This is, needless to say, an extreme view; Nicholas has just come back from a massively expensive and emotionally somewhat catastrophic jaunt in the outer world. But this *kind* of view of the regiment persists as a point of return throughout the novel; in the words of Professor Prince Lobanov-Rostovsky, Tolstoy saw that

> 'the regiment in Russia was more than a military unit: it was an organic whole and a kind of alternative home for its members . . . The members were held together by a curious combination of harsh discipline and nearly democratic paternalism, which blended rather incongruously but effectively to reflect the national temperament in both its strength and weakness.'[6]

The sense of the regiment is pervasive in all the writers of the period, and it was deliberately fostered by a number of serving officers in works intended to be read by the army of their time — notably General Ivan Skobelev (father of the 'hero of Plevna', and often referred to as 'the Pasha') and A. Pogossky, who had served for many years in the ranks.[7] Such works are interesting in that they suggest an ideal of soldierly conduct and comradeship which, in a sense, stands independent of political loyalties; at the same time it is only fair to note that both Skobelev and Pogossky stress devotion to the Emperor as an essential part of the soldier's vocation. When the notion of the regiment is challenged the terms of the challenge themselves reflect the institution's power. To take the case of Tolstoy: the regimental ideology expressed in *War and Peace* is challenged both explicitly and implicitly in

Anna Karenina. In *War and Peace* the regiment, however indirectly, is an image of the *mir*, the community of all Russia that the novel is largely about. *Anna Karenina*, on the other hand, ends with Levin as a solitary figure at variance with what seems, for the moment, the universal expression of such an ideology: 'He wanted to ask why, if public opinion is an infallible judge, is a Revolution and a Commune not as lawful as the movement in favour of the Slavs?' Even so this is not, I feel, a rejection of all the premises on which Tolstoy based his approval of the regiment as a unit. The officers in Vromsky's regiment are often unsympathetically portrayed, but that a feeling for regimental life remained alive in Tolstoy is evident; the kind of group unity it represented was still an ideal of a sort. Before the ultimate challenge Tolstoy, like Levin, faltered. Certainly he never pushed the pacifism of his later years to its obvious conclusion, and he was always liable to recall with emotion the comradeship he had experienced in regimental life, just as he was prepared to reproach the defenders of Port Arthur, after their defeat, with the view that the 'men of Sevastopol' would have done better. It is probable, also, that his habit of command, which he never wholly abandoned, was a product of his army days; he gave up his hopes of being a general in the army, he once jestingly said, to be a general in literature — but the joke is given an ironic twist when we find Chekhov writing to Suvorin that Tolstoy is 'as despotic as a general and as lacking in consideration', even though he qualifies this view by remarking that it is true of 'every great sage'. If we wish to find a detailed criticism of regimental life we must turn to the pages of Kuprin, and even there we encounter anomalies.

Kuprin was, to a quite remarkable degree, the victim of Russian military institutions. The circumstances of his induction into them are in themselves revealing. His family had fallen on hard times, and the only possible way of obtaining an education for the boy was to put him, at the age of eleven, into one of the military cadet colleges. These were simply secondary schools, but run on military lines and with a regimen that included drill, parades and the guard room. They did not lead directly to a commission, as it was necessary to serve for a probationary period as a *yunker* (that is, as a military cadet as we now understand it in Britain) before this could be obtained. Kuprin recorded his experiences in the military school at length in his novel *Cadets* (1900), originally conceived as part of a longer work, to be entitled *Breaking Point*, which he eventually completed with the publication of *Young Officers* in 1928.[8] *The Duel* is in some respects an interlude between these works. All three are autobiographical, although it would be wrong to regard Romashov, the hero of *The Duel*, as being at all an accurate self-portrait of the author.

The Duel is a finer work than the other two military novels because

it is given a concise and economical form. It opens characteristically:
'The VI company's evening classes were drawing to an end, and the
junior officers kept glancing at their watches with ever increasing frequency and frustration. The soldiers were receiving instruction in the
regulations governing guard duty . . .' The novel proceeds to expose
the casual brutalities of military life, the 'use of hands' (which could
amount to beating up) by the officers, the futility and boredom of a
third-rate regiment in a dead-end provincial town. Romashov has daydreams of prowess and glory, fantasies which today have resonances
that were absent when they were first published:

> 'Horrible bloody hostilities against Germany and Austria were under
> way. A vast battlefield . . . dead bodies . . . bursting grenades . . .
> death . . . blood. It is the decisive battle of the campaign . . . The last
> reserves are being thrown into the struggle . . . But Colonel Shulgovich is desperately nervous . . . He shuts his eyes . . . He shuts his
> eyes, trembles, turns pale . . . Now he has already made the sign to
> the bugler to sound the retreat. The soldier lifts the bugle to his lips
> . . . but at that very instant, from behind the hill, appears on a
> frothing Arab stallion the divisional commander's chief-of-staff,
> Colonel Romashov.'

This is, as Kuprin intended it to be, splendid *Boy's Own Paper* stuff,
but the irony is bitter indeed. Against a background of day-to-day military procedure, described in great detail, Romashov is entrapped in
futilities that are partly of his own making, but in large measure of
other people's. He becomes involved with a regimental wife who, whilst
she is apparently happy to flirt with him, is nevertheless deeply involved in her husband's future: 'You know perfectly well that Volodia
didn't invent gunpowder, but he's honest, hardworking and brave. Just
let him get a staff appointment and I'll promise I'll make him a brilliant
career.' He has plenty of complaints about the way in which the army
is run, the stupidity of generals, and all the usual grouses of the junior
officer, but his problem is essentially personal. A drunken comrade
tells him: 'And if they command us to die we'll die, God damn it!'
Romashov replies, miserably: 'We will, but what's dying? It's nothing.
It's living that hurts me, living . . .' In other words, Romashov's problem cannot be attributed simply to the environment in which, as is
admitted by several characters in the novel, there have recently been
considerable changes. These changes, though they are not necessarily
approved by the relaters, the reader is likely to regard as beneficial.
Much time is spent on the education of the soldiers; soldiers' complaints are investigated more thoroughly; there has been a gradual
melioration of conditions of service. Such reforms were in fact instituted at the time of which Kuprin writes, and many of them are

attributable to the interest shown by Nicholas II in the lot of the common soldier.[9] In *The Duel* the main obstacle to their successful furtherance is the total lack of enthusiasm for them amongst some of the officers. It is a complaint continually echoed in military memoirs of the period.[10]

Romashov's protest is against the superficial futility of army life in peacetime; it is not directed at the failings of the Russian military specifically. But, even whilst his revulsion is at its height, a fresh spasm of military activity can weaken his resolve to leave, the glance of a general at a review can make him think to himself: 'The eyes of the fighting general lighted with joy on the slim figure of the young ensign.' And in this very review the fact that the army could aim for virtue, even though it did not attain it, is strongly emphasised. It spells disaster for the regiment that: 'the tiredness of the intimidated soldiers, the pointless cruelty of the NCOs, the dull, mechanical, uninspired attitude of the officers to their duties — all this emerged clearly during the review.' The regiment is a bad regiment, and that is made quite clear in the book. It is Romashov's fate that the local ideal which he has worked for with renewed interest should be judged worthless; the greater whole — the army as represented by the divisional general — demonstrates how short of that ideal the regiment has fallen.

It will be seen from this that, contrary to accepted opinion, *The Duel* is not an anti-militarist novel; it is a novel about a confused and disturbed officer in an admittedly poor regiment. It could even be argued cogently, though not perhaps entirely convincingly, that the theme of the novel embodied a plea for military reform. But Kuprin was not a propagandist — which is why he was never an anti-militarist in the usual sense. He was concerned to describe what he had observed and experienced. The core of his criticism is revealed by two references to the army officers who patronise the brothels described in his other well known (though much less artistically successful) novel, *Yama (The Pit)*. There the officers visiting Anna Markova's establishment are represented as frightened of losing caste in front of the girls and the proprietress, and one of a party of students is at pains to point out to his fellows that 'we aren't army officers who've got to cover up the stupidity of every one of our colleagues'. The comradeship of the regiment has become the oppressive and deadening tyranny of convention. This Kuprin conveys to us in an accurate and unremitting picture of military life — and I know of no equivalent of this in English literature.

The accuracy of his portrayal can be demonstrated from the writings of a man who in many respects could hardly have been more of a contrast to Kuprin, Petr Nikolaevich Krasnov. Kuprin left the army as a lieutenant with only a few kopecks in his pocket, to become a tramp and casual labourer.[11] Krasnov rose to the rank of general and of ataman of the Cossacks, played an active part in the defence of the Provisional Government against the Bolsheviks, and finally emerged as the counter-revolutionary leader of the Don Cossacks. In due course, though before the final White defeat, he went into exile in Berlin and eventually, in his seventies, took command of the Cossack forces serving under the Nazis in the Second World War. He was hanged in Moscow in 1946.12 I hold no brief for his dealings with Hitler; what is of interest is his career between the wars, when he wrote a large number of novels, two of which – *From Double Eagle to Red Flag* (1925) and *To Understand is to Forgive* (1927) (the title, I should point out, is ironical in intention) – have both literary merit and a serious documentary value. A certain Staff Captain K. Popov went a little far, however, when he proposed a comparison between *From Double Eagle to Red Flag* and *War and Peace*.13 The hero of Krasnov's earlier novel is Alexandr Nikolaevich Sablin, who in the course of the book rises from cadet to general. There is, as may be anticipated, a good deal of heart-searching – some of it perceptive, some of it facile – about the causes of the Revolution. Krasnov is at pains to stress the decadence of the upper classes, their increasing commercial involvements, their dabblings in the occult, and the concomitant influence of the 'dark forces' round the throne. But, though his affection for the army comes across on every page, he is also convinced that there was a great deal of decadence in the army as well, a lack of professionalism (Tolstoy's complaint, and, as we have seen, implicit in Lermontov also) and far too much stupidity and brutality. The last point links him with Kuprin; indeed, some of his remarks about young officers could well have been written by Kuprin and it is no coincidence that when, at the end of *From Double Eagle to Red Flag*, Sablin is taken by the Bolsheviks back to his old house in an attempt to persuade him to lend his military expertise to the Red Army, it is a volume of Kuprin which he picks out of his bookcase and reads.

At the crisis of *From Double Eagle to Red Flag* it becomes obvious that, for Sablin, his regiment means more than his country. In this respect there is a comparison to be made with *War and Peace*, a comparison that reveals an important distinction. In *War and Peace* the regiment is a microcosm of the country. In Krasnov's book it has become self-contained. An incident in his other worthwhile novel, *To Understand is to Forgive*, makes this plain. The hero is once more a general, and caught up in the Revolution and Civil War, but, unlike Sablin, the Bolsheviks manage to induce him to fight for them. The novel throws much interesting light on rightist politics in the period, particularly on the failure of many conservative officers to throw in their lot with the Whites:

'If it meant suffering and fighting for the emperor, for the true faith, the traditions of centuries, the fundamental pillars of our great Russia, I understand how we could all gladly sacrifice our lives for the cause. But all there is now is Lenin, Chernov, Avksentiev, Chaykovsky, Denikin and so forth. What do you think is going to happen if Denikin wins? Endless speech-making and squabbling will break out once again, there will be lists of candidates, ballot-boxes hurriedly run up out of cigarette cartons, elections, meetings, fights. There is absolutely nothing to choose from, in fact.'

General Kusskov, the hero, finally decides to leave the Reds and to try and get through to Yudenich's army, which has now reached the full extent of its thrust against Petrograd — an advance that, in reality, came close to success. Kusskov hangs around at the improvised front, waiting his moment while the Red Guards are mustered to defend the city. Looking at them, he notes how:

'Cigarette smoke curled above their grey peaked caps and soft felt hats. There was none of the strong healthy smell of Russian infantry, a mixture of leather, boot grease, cheap tobacco and the human animal, a smell so familiar that he had grown to like it. They smelt of something stale and rank.'

The comment is perhaps a little startling, and suggests an olefactory interpretation of the Revolution: it has to be seen against the admission that Kusskov had only 'come to like' the smell of the Imperial Army soldiers. But there is, in the nature of the observation, evidence enough of affection for that army, extending, in this instance, to a side of it which foreign visitors found unpleasant. The main point to be made, though, is that Krasnov likes the common people when they have been drafted and disciplined, but isn't prepared to accept them as they are when this process has passed them by. At the conclusion of *From Double Eagle to Red Flag* Sablin is quite explicit that the end of his regiment means more to him than does the end of Imperial Russia — not, as he admits, that he could imagine the one without the other. The observation is testimony to the accuracy of the view of the strength and importance of group loyalties that is now a commonplace amongst students of morale, and is in some cases deliberately fostered in military training institutions. It ties in with the impression that we receive from a book covering the same period, which is perfectly straightfoward autobiography.

This is General A. A. Ignatyev's *Fifty Years in the Service*, a memoir by a soldier who, after a career in the Guards and service as a military attaché in Paris in the First World War, joined the Red Army and eventually rose to the rank of general.[14] Ignatyev's is a fascinating document, and is self-evidently truthful. It has, of course, a contemporary political relevance since one of its objects is to stress the continuity of Ignatyev's service — the Revolution is of enormous significance, but Ignatyev's record of service establishes a perspective; both before and afterwards he served *Russia*. As a result there are certain oddities, most of which can be attributed to the author's desire both to paint an accurate picture of the Imperial Army with all its faults and to imply that the army of Russia, whether Imperial or Red, marches on, the guardian of the country from its foreign foes. It matches with Stalin's reinstatement of ranks and epaulettes and his refoundation of the Guards regiments. Thus from Ignatyev we receive an equally strong impression of the importance of the regiment, and of its cohesion, even though there is a deliberate attempt to see it from the outside. Many of his criticisms contain the implied presumption that such-and-such an idle officer's conduct was deplorable, not merely on general ethical principles, but because it let down the unit to which he belonged, the regiment. There can be little doubt, in fact, that regiments stay surprisingly the same, whatever government may ask them to march in whichever direction; the units portrayed in the *Red Cavalry* stories of Isaac Babel (1920-30), and even in Ostrovsky's appalling but socially important *How the Steel was Tempered* (1933), are in some respects similar in atmosphere to an Imperial regiment, despite the utterly different terms in which they are described.

Ignatyev did not believe that the reintroduction of epaulettes and ranks in the Soviet army, nor the reintroduction of the title 'Guards regiment', meant that there should be any further return to the customary observances of the old army. But he certainly adhered to the view that there was a remarkable similarity between that which was best in the old army and that which was best in the new. His account is important both for its assertion of continuing traditions and for the way in which it corroborates the fictional versions; his criticisms are reminiscent of those offered by Kuprin — he takes exception, for instance, to officers who, whilst on manoeuvres, end up with their platoons sheltering in signal boxes because 'the weather is too cold'! The ground of this objection is not that the officer in question was an aristocrat, but that he was a bad officer; Ignatyev (himself a member of the nobility) is perhaps at his most embarrassed when dealing with men such as Mannerheim and Wrangel (both of whom were his contemporaries) who were politically unacceptable but at the same time undeniably efficient soldiers. In these cases he is driven to resort to gossip in order to blacken them. In short, there can be little doubt that, if Ignatyev had encountered Tolstoy's story of the officer who struck an exhausted man who fell out, and was asked by a comrade: 'How can you strike that man? Have you not read the New Testament?', he would have been inclined to answer, with the officer, 'Have *you* not read Army Orders?' His whole memoir is testimony to an abiding tradition, and to the fact that Russian military literature represents inside views.

The endeavour of this account has been to isolate a very few of the things that it tells us about the conflict between the amateur and professional officers, the strength of feeling for the regiment, and the tendency of members of groups to identify with those groups even when, in many respects. they are out of sympathy with them. Close scrutiny would bring to light a great deal more. Some of this would apply to Russia only. It seems likely, for example, that the change in feeling for the regiment evident in a comparison between Tolstoy and Kuprin is not merely a reflection of the difference in temperament and circumstances between these two writers. After the early death of the younger Skobelev in 1881, one of his officers said (according to V. I. Nemirovich-Dantchenko):

> 'Do you know, he is the last! A comrade, a true comrade, though I was but a lieutenant and he a full general. There will be none like that any more. This is a middle class age. Everyone is more or less of a lackey; if he is promoted to be body-servant he will look down on the coachman.'[15]

This anonymous soldier's reaction was echoed, in different ways, by many others, and a modern historian of the Russian army has pointed out that no general in the years to come was ever revered as Slobelev was.[16] The point is a substantial one, and it fits with the literary evidence. It seems that with the coming of compulsory military service in 1874, and with the less easily debatable (because very gradual) but no less important process by which 'middle class' careers were opened up for the educated classes, the nature of the officer caste did undergo a change. The profession degenerated; no general who followed Skobelev possessed anything approaching his breadth of knowledge and sympathies, embracing both science and the arts, and none lived on such familiar terms with the world at large. Alexander II may have been, in General Andolenko's words, the liberator 'as much of the soldier as the serf', but his reforms, in conjunction with the other changes in Russian society, altered the nature and outlook of the officer corps.

Much Russian military fiction, however, has a general applicability, and I would contend that no other European literature contains anything like an equivalent record of army life, and none of it is of the same quality. That it is necessary to adduce examples such as de Vigny in order to counter this argument is a fact eloquent in itself. De Vigny is concerned far more with the ideal of service and the possibility of a code of morality based on honour than with a close and realistic description of army life. His method is symbolic, and his *Servitude et grandeur militaires*, in so far as it is autobiographical, has to be concerned with the spiritual rather than the concrete. The Russians, because the involvement of a sensitive writer with the army was not that anomaly in Russia that it was beginning to seem in nineteenth-century France, were able to describe the military life rather than their narrowly personal reactions to it; it could be argued that de Vigny is the more sophisticated, but it could equally well be advanced that the Russians are the more objective.

There is, in Western Europe, plenty of writing about war, but precious little of merit about regular armies. English literature yields very little; to find anything in the nineteenth century even of slight value we have to turn either to Kipling (a special case) or to Ireland and the work, at best minor and always avowedly comic in intent, of Charles Lever. Lever is the poor offering we can make, and it is significant that he is representative of an unusual class who, for economic and social reasons peculiar to West Britain were forced to send into the army men who in other circumstances would have found vocations of a different kind. The twentieth century has seen a number of accessions to the body of military literature contributed as a result of the enlistment of professional authors during the two periods of national emergency. The names of Ford Madox Ford, Evelyn Waugh and Anthony Powell come to mind. These accounts of army life have been, in their various ways, outstanding. But they have represented the unusual circumstances of a wartime, part-conscripted army, for all that they have contained flashes of insight that illuminate the conditions of regular service. It ir noteworthy, too, that all three authors have been concerned to represent the influence of a dramatised military role on their principal characters — this is very evidently so with Guy Crouchback and his prayer at the crusader's tomb before he leaves for the war. Anthony Powell has actually embodied in the three military movels of his *Music of Time* sequence[17] an examination of just this process, an examination that displays a full awareness of its literary ancestry. De Vigny is explicitly and tellingly adverted to, whilst — and it is a measure of the depth and subtlety of the work, a depth of which its critics seem largely unaware — Nick Jenkins is aware of some of General Skobelev's more remarkable pronouncements.

The last point takes us full circle. In Russia peculiar circumstances forced into the regular army men who, in other countries, would scarcely have dreamed of entering it. Amongst such men there were inevitably those who would, in due course, emerge as writers. In consequence we have an imaginative and interpretative literature about the occasions and emotions of regular soldiering such as is to be found in no other country. It tells of boredom, minimal motivation, loyalties conceived narrowly in terms of a group, vast failures of comprehension (the portrayal of the other ranks is a subject in itself), and the deliberate adoption of roles.

All of these things are of great relevance to any study of military and national attitudes, and deserve far more attention than they have generally received. Their applicability, certainly, has not altered in the past century, despite the apparent revolutions of attendant circumstance.

Notes

1. Maude translation. Translations from authors other than Tolstoy are my own.
2. For this episode see Henri Troyat, *Tolstoy*, Harmondsworth, 1970, pp. 100-20.
3. John Bayley (*Tolstoy and the Novel*, London, 1966, pp. 15-20) discusses some of the general implications of this aspect of the career of so many Russian writers.
4. For this see N. V. Shelgunov, L. P. Shelgunova, M. L. Mikaylov, *Vospominaniya*, 2 vols., Moscow, 1967, I, pp. 71-2.
5. One quotation is from Vladimir Nabokov's edition of *Eugene Onegin* (4 vols., New York, 1964, III, p. 283).
6. Introduction to M. Lyons, *The Russian Imperial Army, a bibliography*, Stanford, 1968, p. xiv.
7. General C. R. Andolenko, *Histoire de l'Armée Russe*, Paris, 1967, p. 257.
8. Texts are from the *Sobranie sochineniy*, ed K. G. Paustovsky, 6 vols., Moscow, 1957-8.
9. An anticipatably enthusiastic account may be found in Professor Eltchaninow, *La Règne de S. M. L'Empereur Nicolas II*, trans. Madame la Comtesse de Hohenfelsen, Paris, 1913, pp. 71-87. This semi-official publication celebrated the three-hundredth anniversary of the Romanovs.
10. Notably those of A. A. Brussilov, (*Moy vospominaniya*, Moscow, 1929), Vasily Gourko, (*Memories and Impressions, 1914-1917*, London, 1918), and Gustav Mannerheim, (*Memoirs*, London, 1953).
11. For a good account of Kuprin's character, see K. Chukovsky, *Sovremenniky*, Moscow, 1967, pp. 162-93. A literary assessment may be found in Charles Ledve, *Trois romanciers russes*, Paris, 1937.
12. Krasnov, inexplicably, awaits his biographer. There is interesting material in Gregory P. Tschebotarioff, *Russia My Native Land*, New York, 1964, pp. 141-78. For his activities in 1917 see *Arkiv russkoy revolutsiy*, vol. I, 2nd edn, Berlin, 1922, pp. 97-190.
13. K. Popov, *Voina i mir' i 'Ot dvuglavago orla k krasnomu znamei' v svete nashih dney*, Paris, 1934.
14. A. A. Ignatyev, *Pyatdesyat let v stroyu*, 2 vols., Moscow, 1955; originally published, from 1944 onwards, as magazine articles.
15. V. I. Nemirovitch-Dantchenko, *Personal Reminiscences of General Skobeleff*, trans. E. A. Brayley Hodgetts, London, 1884, p. 343.
16. General Andolenko, *op. cit.*, p. 280.
17. *The Valley of Bones* (1964); *The Soldier's Art* (1966); *The Military Philosophers* (1968).

3 MAKING AN ARMY REVOLUTIONARY: FRANCE 1815-48

Douglas Porch

Despite the vast amount of research on the revolutionary movement during and after the French Revolution, the problems and mechanics of the revolutionary movement in the army have been largely ignored.

The French army in the early years of the July Monarchy is especially suited for a study of revolution and political activism. Bequeathed largely intact to the conservative Restoration in 1815, its revolutionary origins, intense patriotism and large contingent of ex-imperial officers and NCOs made it a potential hotbed of political opposition.

The years between 1815 and 1823 witnessed several widely publicised, if abortive, military insurrections led by ex-Napoleonic soldiers, including the four sergeants of La Rochelle and General Berton's 1822 uprising. Though no military conspiracies were reported after the 1823 Spanish campaign, it was widely believed that, just beneath the surface, the army was simmering with political discontent.

The events of July 1830 in Paris are well known. Provincial garrisons, removed from the pressures of insurrection, looked on apathetically as the Bourbons were forced out of France. Yet repercussions from the Revolution demonstrate the relationship between governmental instability, indiscipline and republican activity in the army. In many provincial towns, news of the Revolution was greeted with unrestrained joy. Large crowds gathered in Metz, Strasbourg, Bordeaux, Caen, Lyon, Clermont-Ferrand and many other towns to await news from Paris. Opposition leaders demanding the resurrection of the National Guard and that the tricolour replace the white flag immediately challenged the authority of local government officials; local hierarchies either resigned or teetered dangerously on the brink of collapse.

The breakdown of civil discipline also tainted the army. Faced with a revolutionary *fait accompli* and an armed citizenry, most commanders hesitated between duty and their sympathy for the Revolution or their impotence before the aroused town. This refusal to assert authority proved fatal to military discipline.

As news of the Revolution threw garrison towns into turmoil, and as officers nervously awaited orders from Paris, NCOs wasted little time in disrupting their regiments. In most cases they seized as a pretext for revolt their superior's refusal to let them wear the tricoloured cockade, which the National Guard had taken up immediately, until orders arrived from Paris. For this reason many NCOs, egged on by local republicans who were buying drinks and passing out money, reasoned that their officers were holding the regiments in check until the Bourbons could consolidate their forces and retake Paris. Consequently, many NCOs and soldiers stationed near Paris deserted to ride to Paris and protect the Revolution.

On 3 August, a sergeant in the sixth chasseurs at Givet ordered 200 men to saddle up and prepare to ride on the capital. The colonel quickly ordered the city gates closed, halted the group and demanded where they were going. They answered that they were riding to Paris themselves because he refused to take them there. The colonel objected that he could not lead them to Paris without orders, but they insisted that he had received orders and was holding them back. They also accused him of plotting to abandon them. Despite the colonel's protests, eighty-four NCOs and soldiers broke past him and galloped for Paris.[1]

This scene was repeated elsewhere, especially in cavalry regiments, not, as Rémusat suggested, because NCOs particularly resented the aristocratic officers who dominated that arm but because mounted soldiers found it easier to reach the capital.

Reports of trouble in 32 out of the 148 French regiments reached the War Ministry. It is certain that these reports understate the real extent of unrest. Later estimates of desertion were much greater than contemporary records suggest. According to a report drawn up in 1841, army strength, which stood at 223,073 officers and men in January 1830, plummeted to 183,311 in August, a loss of 40,000 men.[2]

Yet the deserters rode to Paris for reasons other than to save the Revolution. The prospect of higher pay and a promotion promised those who joined the Paris National Guard played a decisive part in the decision of NCOs and soldiers to desert. A soldier who received 45 centimes a day was clearly attracted by the daily wage of 1 franc 50 centimes supposedly offered by the Paris National Guard. The colonel of the sixth chasseurs claimed that republican promises of higher pay and the possibility of promotion in the National Guard were behind the Givet revolt.[3]

Yet the War Minister believed that the mutiny in the ranks could have been prevented had the officers acted firmly to prevent civil indiscipline from spreading to the garrison. Faced with an unstable political situation and without orders from Paris, officers hesitated to take strong measures for which they could later be held accountable. The future Marshal Canrobert, at Lyon in 1830, concluded that the bravest soldiers often deserted in the face of civil war: 'The soldier dreads civil war', he wrote. 'He does not know if the cause he is defending will be victorious, or if perhaps tomorrow he will be serving the insurgents . . . He becomes restless, manifesting a lethargy and distrust which sometimes leads him to desert, to disobey and panic.'[4] In a letter to the Minister of the Interior, the Strasbourg prefect deplored the inability of officers to put down indiscipline in the garrison following the revolution: 'These old soldiers, so brave on the battlefield, rarely show courage in a civil crisis.'[5] Lieutenant La Motte Rouge corroborated the atmosphere of mistrust in the Lille garrison:

> 'We met, we eyed each other, we conversed without daring to utter a candid opinion on the situation or on its likely outcome. I was struck by the expressions of uncertainty and anticipation which marked every face and many of my friends. Normally open discussion gave way to caution, to a defiance born of the fear of compromising oneself by an ambiguous word or sentence.'[6]

As long as the government remained unstable, the army was continually threatened by republican activists who took advantage of the officers' weakened authority. In November 1831, Marshal Castellane noted the adverse effects of governmental instability on military discipline. He pointed out that officers were wary of taking decisive action, for junior officers and NCOs often denounced the strict disciplinarian as a Carlist, a partisan of the deposed Charles X. Consequently, most officers turned a blind eye to insubordination.[7] He pointed out that governmental instability had encouraged indecision even on the ministerial level and accused the War Minister, ex-Napoleonic Marshal Soult, of not punishing indiscipline for fear of revolution. Rémusat also noted that Soult maintained his connections with the Left in case the government fell.[8] Several colonels claimed that the lack of clear directives from the War Ministry had undermined their authority and ability to act rigorously against mutineers. Faced with a complete governmental breakdown both on the national and local level combined with the interruption of pay on which soldiers depended for their daily rations, officers abdicated before the wave of patriotism and indiscipline which swept through the ranks. They went underground until the political situation was stable enough to allow them to re-establish discipline without fear of political reprisals. Consequently, republican activity in the army increased in direct proportion to governmental instability.

The Revolution in the army quickly entered a second and more prolonged phase as many NCOs, conscious that the authority of the officers was undermined, began to denounce their superiors as Carlists and counter-revolutionaries in an attempt to have them suspended and to take their places. Indiscipline and denunciation were so widespread following the Revolution that virtually every regiment experienced some trouble. 'A Carlist', the saying went, 'is someone who has a job someone else wants.'9 Here begins a study of the special position of the French NCO which caused him to play such an active role in the July Revolution and subsequent republican activity in the army after 1830.

The revolutionary NCO is a phenomenon peculiar to the post-revolutionary French army. Hoping to democratise the class structured army of the *ancien régime*, revolutionary governments worked to open the officer corps to the lower classes. To facilitate direct promotion from sergeant to second lieutenant, they struck down the 1780 ordinance which restricted the officer corps to the nobility. As St-Cyr was too small to fill the yearly officer quota, most French officers came up through the ranks in the infantry and cavalry, though the artillery continued to be dominated by school trained men. In 1832, Marshal Soult pointed out that of 4,489 men commissioned as second lieutenants between 1821 and 1831, 2,537 were promoted through the ranks and 1,952 through military schools.[10] Well over half of the officers were ex-NCOs.

This promotion system had a peculiar effect on the French army. Most armies were stratified according to class, with the soldier's career terminating at the relative position of his class in the military hierarchy; lower class soldiers could hope to be sergeants or sergeant-majors, middle class officers ended their careers as captains or majors, while aristocrats hoped for a higher command. Each soldier realised that his ambitions were limited by his social class. The revolutionary application of the promotion system in the French army broke down class barriers and weakened the traditional social authority of the military hierarchy: a lower middle class soldier now aspired to a commission and was no longer content with a lower rank. Consequently, the NCO 'class' was fluid and socially unstable. It welcomed the prospect of political turmoil which undermined the officers' authority and created opportunity for promotion.

As Napoleon recognised when he observed that every French soldier carried a marshal's baton in his knapsack, the post-revolutionary French army offered lower middle class soldiers an excellent opportunity to improve their social position. The ambition of these NCOs explains their indiscipline and the large-scale denunciations following the Revolution. Republicans directed their propaganda almost exclusively at NCOs while officials repeatedly advised the War Ministry to make every effort to ensure NCO loyalty to the Orleans government and especially by giving frequent promotion.

Of those soldiers cited by name in reports to the War Minister for republican activity under the July Monarchy, 18 per cent were sergeant-majors, 51 per cent were sergeants, 14 per cent were corporals and only 17 per cent were privates. The vast majority of military republicans were NCOs.[11]

NCOs continued to lead efforts to spread republicanism in the army after 1830. They stood to gain by indiscipline and confusion in the army and therefore were attracted to the opposition, as in 1830. But the emergence of the tough conservative chief minister Casimir Périer and the subsequent re-establishment of governmental stability revealed the weakness of republican dependence on NCOs: an NCO-led revolution was successful only if officer authority was already undermined by a weak and vacillating government. Rebellious NCOs seldom held out against determined authority nor were they able to persuade soldiers to follow them. Because they were primarily concerned for their own well-being, they quickly gave way before the authority of military discipline.

The special position of the artillery

The most rebellious NCOs were those in the artillery. 'It is noticeable', wrote the Minister of the Interior in 1840, 'that it is always artillery soldiers who have followed the lead given by the most radical sector of the population.'[12] It was here too that the minority of rebellious officers was most heavily concentrated.

The artillery,[13] which consisted of fourteen regiments and a battalion of bridge builders in 1835, was notorious for its republican sympathies. It accounted for only 7 per cent of army strength. Yet between 1823 and 1830, 33 per cent of the incidents of political unrest concerned the artillery. Between the July Revolution and 1840, every artillery regiment was cited in reports to the War Minister for disloyalty.

The traditional explanations of the artillery's political opposition are by now familiar. The aristocracy shunned the artillery when firearms first appeared, prefering the 'honourable' combat of the cavalry and infantry. The artillery, therefore, at first attracted only middle class officers who were not unwilling to challenge the established order. Second, the artillery was associated with science, technology and industry — which had set in motion vast social and economic change. Vagts sums up the aristocracy's traditional hatred of the artillery: 'The resentment of the nobleman against the artillery was a part of that large heritage carried over from feudal times into modern warfare, which included the most variegated complex of antiquated sentiments, convictions, valuations and a general disinclination for technological progress.'[14] For these reasons, the artillery was the arm most responsive to and indeed most eager for social change.

On closer examination, however, these two facts alone do not explain the rebelliousness of the artillery under the July Monarchy.

With the Revolution, the artillery acquired new prestige. As aristocrats left France and the army, the artillery lost its stigma of social inferiority and revolutionary generals with inexperienced troops became increasingly dependent on it. On 16 brumaire, year VI (6 November 1787) the War Minister, General Scherer, placed the artillery first in the order of march, followed by the infantry and cavalry.[15] The Ecole Polytechnique was established in 1793 and the artillery began to furnish the army with famous generals. Bonaparte, of course, was an artillery officer. Clermont-Tonnerre, Archbishop of Toulouse and War Minister under the Restoration, was a Polytechnician and held an artillery commission; Marmont, commander of the Paris garrison in July 1830, was commissioned in the artillery; Baron d'Hautpoul, commander of the Ecole Royale d'Etat Major under the Restoration, and the school's Inspector-General Desprez were classmates at the Polytechnique. General Foy, a leader of the parliamentary opposition in the Restoration, and Marshal Gouvion-Saint-Cyr, architect of the 1818 army reform, were artillery officers. Under the July Monarchy, General Valée, an artillery general, was appointed Governor-General of Algeria, while other officers such as General Cavaignac also staked out brilliant careers from the ranks of the artillery.

The resignation of many aristocratic officers after 1830 substantially reduced the class differentiation among the three arms which had been assumed to be a major cause of the artillery's insubordination. This class difference, while applicable to the German army which was organised along strict class lines, does not apply to the French army.

A tradition of political opposition undoubtedly existed in the artillery and among graduates of the Ecole Polytechnique. But to explain the republican bias of the artillery satisfactorily, we must look deeper into its organisation and situation.

Republicans often sought to exploit regimental and personal problems for political ends. This was especially true in the artillery, where young officers leaving the Ecole Polytechnique and Metz's Ecole d'Application were financially insecure. Baron Pelletier, commander of the Ecole d'Application, complained in 1837 that unavoidable debts incurred by the students were a major reason for the school's notorious republicanism. In an inspection report, he pointed out that most Polytechnicians came from families forced to make financial sacrifices to send them to college. After graduating from the Ecole Polytechnique, they were placed on half pay until term began at Metz. They therefore arrived at Metz owing at least 400 francs and with little hope of paying off their debts but rather certain to incur new ones.

General Pelletier's contention is born out by the archives of the Ecole Polytechnique. Of 42 students disciplined for republican activity between 1830 and 1834, only 2 were sons of men wealthy enough to appear on the electoral roll. Ten were sons of minor civil servants, 10 were sons of small proprietors, 7 of army officers, 4 of lawyers, 4 of merchants, 2 of engineers, 2 of naval officers and one student's father was a teacher. We can conclude that most Polytechnicians involved in republican activity were from middle class backgrounds and unable to build a career from family wealth or connections. The army and the civil service were therefore the most likely career choices. In most cases their pay — a potential source of discontent — was their only source of income.

A young artillery officer's financial worries did not end with his departure from Metz. After graduating in the spring, he was given an extended leave while awaiting his orders for assignment to a regiment. These orders arrived usually in July but some students received their assignments as late as September. General Pelletier pointed out that though the students were free to go home, few could afford to do so. Most of them were forced to await their assignment in Metz for five or six months on a salary of fifty francs a month. He underlined the political importance of preventing officers from accumulating debts by pointing out that most officers involved in political activity since 1815, including several recent Metz graduates involved in Louis Napoleon's 1836 *coup d'état*, were deep in debt. And, indeed, examples of debt ridden officers involved in political activity under the July Monarchy are numerous. The relationship between debt and republicanism was apparent to others in the army and inspecting generals often dismissed officers in debt. It is interesting to note that artillery regiments were stationed in those areas of France where the cost of living was highest — the large cities and the east.

Of the officers cited for republican activity under the July Monarchy, almost 40 per cent were under thirty. This created a potentially explosive situation, for these young and impoverished officers were especially willing to embrace republicanism.

The prolonged education required of artillery officers also appears to have affected Metz students. Upon graduation from the Ecole Polytechnique, they received the rank of student second lieutenant and settled down for another two years of study at Metz which they normally completed at the age of twenty-two or twenty-three. Though they received the rank and pay of a second lieutenant, they enjoyed few of the privileges. They were still forced to endure the gruelling mental and physical discipline of school life, and although commissioned they were not entitled to salutes and other military courtesies from NCOs and soldiers. While their contemporaries from St-Cyr and those in civilian life were enjoying the advantages and status of their positions, Metz students were still denied even the trappings of responsibility. Judging by the number of requests by the students to be allowed to receive salutes and outher courtesies, this prolonged adolescence was painful to them. Their frustration over their lack of status and responsibility encouraged insubordination and their flirtations with the opposition.

Slow promotion, while an army wide problem, was especially acute in the artillery. The smallest of the three major arms, comprising less than a tenth of army personnel, the artillery had a smaller personnel turnover and consequently fewer opportunities for promotion, a major source of army discontent. Between 1831 and 1841, the artillery lost only 36.3 per cent of its officers or an average of 54.7 men a year. In the same period, the cavalry lost 50.9 per cent or 182.9 officers a year and the infantry 55.3 per cent or 612.9 men a year.[16]

Artillery officers faced other promotional handicaps. At least two thirds of all artillery officers passed through the Ecole Polytechnique and could not expect the same career advantages to follow from their elitist education as could the relatively rare St-Cyrians in the infantry and cavalry. For example, of 179 second lieutenants listed in the 1834 *Annuaire*, only 50 had been promoted through the ranks. The remainder were Polytechnicians. St-Cyrians counted for less than one third of cavalry officers and roughly one fourth of infantry officers.[17]

Also, between 1815 and 1848 an artillery officer had virtually no chance to distinguish himself in the field. Ambitious infantry and cavalry officers could look for rapid promotion in Algeria, but the nature of guerrilla warfare and General Bugeaud's tactics, which called for small, mobile, 'flying columns' designed for long range patrols rather than large scale operations, dictated that the artillery would be used only in defence. Consequently, only 4 per cent of the officers stationed in Algeria in January 1840 belonged to the artillery and those who were sent there could look forward to an uneventful stay. Ambitious artillery and engineering officers, like Cavaignac, La Moricière, Duvivier and Marey-Monge who joined the Zouaves and Chasseurs d'Afrique in Algeria, were forced to transfer to other arms or face the prospect of an unprofitable career. 12.25 per cent of the Polytechnicians who joined the artillery between 1831 and 1841 resigned as opposed to 8.7 per cent of the St-Cyrians who joined the cavalry and only 5.9 per cent who joined the infantry in the same period, indicating that discontent was more widespread in the artillery.[18]

Slow promotion was also a problem for artillery NCOs and soldiers. Although promotion in the infantry and cavalry was slow, one or two years might pass with no promotions at all in the artillery. An 1836 inspection report pointed out that artillery NCOs had had no promotion at all for two years and might be encouraged to join the opposition camp.[19]

Another important consideration in the study of republicanism in the artillery is the location of garrisons. Political opposition in the army depended largely on civilian agents for its propagation; it was rare in areas where the Republican Party was weak, but frequent in garrison towns where the party was strong.

Under the Restoration and July Monarchy, the French left counted a large following among students and young professional men in the 'patriotic' east and in the large cities. 'By drawing a line from Metz to Montpellier', the *Tribune* announced in August 1833, 'you have a republican map of France.' But this map would exclude Paris and other quite large republican centres like Toulouse and Perpignan, where canvassing was frequently reported in the garrisons, and many smaller ones including Rennes, Nantes and Montauban. Opposition activity in the army, on the other hand, was infrequent in the west and extreme south-west.

Of fifteen artillery units in 1835, three were stationed in Strasbourg, two in Metz, two in Toulouse and one each in Paris, Lyon, Besançon, Rennes, Douai, La Fère, Valence and Bourges. Strasboug, Metz, Toulouse, Paris, Lyon and Besançon were all republican strongholds and local republicans were active in the garrisons. The remaining four cities boasted smaller republican societies. Almost three quarters of the artillery regiments were stationed in traditionally republican areas — this is proportionally higher than the other arms — and every regiment was in continual contact with civilian republican societies.

In addition, artillery regiments, owing to the limited number of practice ranges, remained in one station for four to six years, longer than infantry and cavalry regiments which were transferred annually or biannually. This is important for two reasons. First, republicans had plenty of time to canvass in the regiment. Second, as the regiments were recruited locally, they found it easier to recruit among people from their region.

The army was not blind to the disadvantages of a prolonged garrison stay in a republican area and officials frequently requested the transfer of a regiment which had remained too long in one town. A long stay in Strasbourg was particularly damaging to military discipline. Dependent on Germany for much of its trade, the town had a large, liberal commercial middle class. Unlike French cafés, Alsacian brasseries attracted all classes of people who mixed freely. In Strasbourg, soldiers were more likely to mix with this liberal middle class than to confront fist-happy workers who resented the army. The gregarious brasserie afforded republicans the opportunity to establish contacts in the garrison.

Combined with a long garrison stay, the policy of regional recruitment created a dangerous homogeneity among artillery soldiers. The army favoured regional recruitment because local recruits could easily reach their regiments and were less likely to desert because of homesickness. Yet local recruitment had its disadvantages. Republicans could canvass more easily among local recruits, while soldiers from a particular region, like Alsace, could adopt an opposition political doctrine as a sign of regional independence and pride. After a large 1833 Strasbourg demonstration in which civilians joined many officers and soldiers of the battalion of bridge builders to protest against promotional abuses, Colonel Boursaroque obtained permission from the War Minister to close his battalion, which was permanently stationed in Strasbourg, to Alsacians who numbered 221 of 740 men in his force. He complained that they frequently established civilian contacts which undermined discipline.

As many regiments were stationed in Protestant areas such as Strasbourg, Metz and Toulouse, many soldiers in the artillery were Protestants. Religious differences frequently carried over into politics in the Midi and the east, as Protestants often chose republicanism as a means of giving political expression to their traditional religious nonconformity. Many also hoped that a republic would end the social inequality forced on them by Catholic France. Protestants frequently ran their own schools and were usually better educated than their Catholic counterparts. Though it is impossible to ascertain the religious make-up of the regiments, artillery regiments by virtue of their locations probably took in a higher proportion of Protestants.

Most of these soldiers who engaged in political activity in the army, especially in the artillery, were volunteers. In 1835, only one twentieth of the army consisted of volunteers.[20] Yet no less than 65 per cent of soldiers cited in reports to the War Minister for republican activity were volunteers,[21] and inspection reports frequently complained about these men. As career soldiers, they were deeply concerned with regimental issues which directly influenced their careers. Conscripts, on the other hand, thought of themselves as civilians able to return home after three or four years' service and were consequently less interested in military issues.

The proportion of volunteers appears to have been higher in the artillery, largely because it was a relatively sedentary arm and because many regiments were stationed in the east which traditionally furnished large numbers of volunteers. A resident of an artillery garrison could volunteer for the artillery knowing that he would remain close to home for a long time. General Lenoury, the artillery's Inspector-General, complained in 1836 that replacements and volunteers counted for nearly half of artillery soldiers.

Education was another contributory factor in the artillery's republicanism. Because of its technical nature, the artillery had a definite policy of recruiting soldiers with above average intelligence and education. These soldiers, who were more conscious of political and social problems and less content with the *status quo*, were commonly thought more open to republicanism or socialist influence. General Lenoury wrote in 1833 that the intelligence of artillery officers often led to political militancy, and soldiers arrested for political activity frequently were reported to be well educated.

If the relationship between education and political opposition is indisputable, as even contemporaries realised, certainly the artillery as the best educated arm could claim to be the most republican.

Furthermore, as most artillery corps were stationed in the east and the large cities, most of their recruits came from these areas. Paris and the east were the most literate areas in France. Regiments stationed in these areas drew on the educational elite of France, and the artillery, because of its longer garrison stays, recruited a larger proportion of these men. On a purely numerical basis, then, the artillery qualifies as the *arme savante*.

Regiments of any arm stationed in the east and in the cities with active republican societies were affected to some extent by republican propaganda. However, the combination of a long garrison stay in a republican area, regional homogeneity, a high proportion of volunteers, financial problems, many educated and some Protestant soldiers and its dependence on schools, especially the Ecole Polytechnique, increased the incidence of republican opposition in the artillery.

Conclusion

Thus revolutionary tendencies in the French army were the product of factors unique to the French military system. Similarly, the decline of active republicanism, both in the army and in society at large after 1834, may be attributed to specific causes. Following that year's Lyon and Paris uprisings, the government moved to break up political associations and republican leaders — including Cavaignac and Marrast — were jailed or exiled. With Lafayette's death in May 1834 followed by Armand Carrel's in an 1836 duel, the republican leadership fell to pieces.

Republicans therefore went underground and were organised into secret societies by hard-core recolutionaries like Barbes and Blanqui, in whose hands republicanism became a doctrine of revolution and social reform. This alienated moderate liberals who joined Lafitte, Arago and Dupont de l'Eure to work for parliamentary reform.

Two 1834 military reforms also help to explain the return of political tranquillity to the army. In this year, pensions — a major cause of complaint under the Restoration — were increased to a level double and sometimes triple the Restoration figures. They were no longer given on the basis of campaigns fought, as, on this reasoning, twenty years of peace would guarantee most officers only a minimum pension. Officers were now paid a flat sum according to their arm. This increased the security of the officer corps, which no longer felt that a peaceful foreign policy would affect retirement pay. Although the pro-war plank in the Republican Party platform was still attractive, it was no longer essential for an officer's wellbeing.

The second law, protecting officers from the arbitrary or politically motivated dismissals so common under the Revolution, Empire and Restoration, was passed on 19 May. It stipulated that officers could be dismissed only by a commission composed of their peers. The War Minister no longer had the right to dismiss his subordinates. The law was crucial, for it guaranteed the stability and continuity of the army under any regime.

Republican political ideology had in itself only limited appeal for the military and had served as little more than a rallying point for discontent with the conditions of service.[23] The simultaneous repression of the republican movement and reform of the conditions of service brought open political dissent within the army almost to an end. Barely 20 per cent of the incidents of political opposition in the army between 1830 and 1848 occurred after 1836. When the July Monarchy was overthrown in the February Revolution of 1848, no open unrest had been reported in the army for four years.

The significance of the French experience between 1815 and 1848 is that it points up most strongly the importance of internal grievances in making an army revolutionary. Republican ideology had a limited appeal; much more fruitful as sources of dissension and mutiny were the burning issues of pay and promotion — much more important, indeed, than class or social antagonisms imported into the army from society. Armies march on their stomachs, and it is in defence of their most mundane rights and privileges that they will usually be tempted to rebel.

Notes

1. Archives Historiques de la Guerre (henceforth AHG), E^5 1, 10 August 1830.
2. *Ibid.*, Fonds Préval 1948.
3. *Ibid.*, E^5 1, 10 August.
4. Bapst, *Le Maréchal Canrobert*, Paris, 1898, pp. 141-2.
5. Archives Nationales, F^{16} I 159^2, dossier Esmangart.
6. La Motte Rouge, *Souvenirs*, Paris, 1889, Vol. I, p. 303.
7. General B. Castellane, *Journal*, Paris, 1895, Vol. II, pp. 460-1.
8. C. de Rémusat, *Memoires*, Paris, 1858-62, pp. 418-9.
9. P. Thureau-Dangin, *Histoire de la Monarchie de Juillet*, Paris, 1889, Vol. I, p. 86.
10. P. Chalmin, *L'Officier français, 1815-1870*, Paris, 1957, p. 82.
11. Eighty-eight sergeant-majors, 258 sergeants, 70 corporals and 84 privates. This list, compiled from the general correspondence of the war archives, series E^5, can be regarded as only a sample.
12. AHG, E^5 90, 22 October.

13. For a more detailed treatment of the artillery see D. Porch, *Army and Revolution: France 1815-1848*, London, 1974.
14. A. Vagts, *A History of Militarism*, New York, 1959, p. 45.
15. L. Susane, *Histoire de l'artillerie française*, Paris, 1874, p. 237.
16. Devalez de Caffol, *Statistique Militaire*, Paris, 1843, 21e tableau.
17. AHG, Fonds Préval 1948.
18. Devalez, *loc. cit.*, tableaux 17 and 18.
19. AHG, X^d 638.
20. *Sentinelle de l'Armée*, 20 March 1835.
21. 236 volunteers, 38 replacements, 94 conscripts, and 10 had been given their stripes after July 1830 as *recompense national*. This list, compiled from the general correspondence of the war archives, represents only a sample.
22. AHG, X^d 368.
23. For further discussion of this point, see Porch, *op. cit.*

4 TECHNOLOGY AND THE MILITARY MIND: AUSTRIA 1866-1914

Andrew Wheatcroft

The Prussian Ministers of War, it has been remarked, 'regarded every change in the *status quo* as somehow an advance for democracy'.[1] Resistance to change seemed common to most military systems before 1914, for irrespective of their social or political colour, novelty was somehow regarded as peculiarly subversive. Perhaps this may be explained as the result of a settled and well established structure being forced to uproot itself and adapt to new ways, a situation well known in civil life; the military resisted the more strongly because their structure was deeply entrenched in the attitudes of the past. Perhaps it was because much of the pressure for change came from external forces — the self-seeking politician, the cheeseparing bureaucrat more concerned with his paperwork than with national defence — forces which soldiers instinctively distrusted and reacted against. It is therefore important to separate resistance to change *per se* from resistance to the sources from which change emanated. Faced with intrusions from outside, armies resisted instinctively; yet with the passage of time, change could be absorbed. So it was with the great controversy over the admission of bourgeois officers into the closed circle of the officer caste: feverishly opposed at the outset, they were eventually accommodated with little difficulty within the system.

As a test of attitudes towards change, reactions to technology have often, by comparison, seemed attractively value free, revealing a pure obscurantism uninfluenced by other factors. One such stereotype Blimp was Sir Thomas Troubridge,[2] a mid-nineteenth-century British Adjutant-General, who opposed a faster-firing small-arm for the British infantry on the grounds that it would both waste ammunition and undermine discipline; indeed, he devised an elaborate mechanical device to reduce the rate of fire. Upon a foundation of such characters, who could be found in most European armies before 1914, a tissue of reactionary military attitudes can be based. The purpose of this article is to suggest that the issues surrounding technology were not value-free, but, on the contrary, could place a severe strain on the established military system, calling in question its fundamental values. Possibly the main difficulty in generalising about the effects of technical change is that there is no agreement as to what are the effects produced by technological innovation within military organisations, both on the political and social structure of the institution and on its relationship with surrounding civil institutions.

The reception of new technology within any given army (taking armies for my purposes as a representative military institution) seems to depend to a large extent on circumstances peculiar to that institution and its surrounding society. Thus, particular types of innovation might pose severe problems to some armies but could be accepted without demur by others, although the latter might be equally dumbfounded by some other novelty. The discussion of the role and function of cavalry on the field of battle, and the endless debates of the comparative merits of carbine, sword and lance in the three decades before the First World War, illustrate the process.[3] However, it is worth noting one common factor which recurs again and again in case studies of technological advance. Innovation is usually expensive and in most armies money is always short. Because an advancing military technology demanded such large capital sums, and an ever-increasing regular expenditure, it provoked a plethora of angry and usually ill informed discussion. Since civilians controlled the purse strings in most European countries before the First World War, and saw in debates on the military budget a means to sustain their power, soldiers and ministers alike came to dread the conflicts which 'progress' carried in its wake.[4] One suspects that behind the impassioned opposition to a particular development lay a simple matter of cash, and behind the bluff obscurantist exterior of many officers, unconvinced by the blessings of technology, lay an administrator trying to balance his budget.

This case study concerns the Austrian army in the years between 1866 and the outbreak of the First World War. Within the army it has narrowly focused on the changes associated with a developing small-arms technology in a conservative military system. The choice of this particular aspect of technological innovation is not entirely arbitrary, first because it was a field in which Austria was particularly successful, and second, because small-arms were a key political area, for reasons which will be set out later. Naturally, the two aspects were connected: Austria had a dynamic small-arms technology because small-arms were closely connected with national pride and prestige, and even relatively obtuse officers had firm views and prejudices on small-arms development while displaying no interest in any other aspect of technical development. There was no great traditional interest in small-arms, as to some extent there was with the artillery in the higher echelons of the army: the pervasive, if superficial, interest in firearms can be traced to a specific series of events.

The causes of change

1866 was a decisive formative influence in the development of the Austrian army for the following forty years. It was as if the army had seen something nasty in the woodshed and the memory of the event never left it. 1866 was remembered less for the victories of the Italians, on land at Custozza and in the naval battle of Lissa, than for the humiliating campaign in the north against Prussia. The most painful memory, repeated by many of the combatants, was the catastrophic failure of the Austrian infantry against the Prussians armed with the breech-loading Dreyse needle-gun. Count Wilczek, who was serving in the rank of a Jaeger battalion, noted how 'the quick-firing needle-guns played such havoc with us that we did not venture to attack them again'.[5] More expert opinion concurred that the needle-gun was the decisive factor and used it to explain how their confident prediction of Prussia's doom before the outbreak of war had been proved worthless on the battlefield. Certainly, the strategic position had not favoured Prussia, with hostile armies poised around her borders and Austria having the theoretical advantage of interior lines of communication if she attacked through Bohemia. Even if many of the smaller states of the German Confederation had tiny armies, Saxony possessed very effective forces, and Bavaria made up in numbers what she lacked in offensive spirit. When Prussia crushed her enemies in a matter of weeks, against the odds, reasons were quickly manufactured to explain the miracle. Two were favoured: first, that the Austrian commander Benedek had failed miserably, and second, that the dreaded needle-gun overturned the normal balance of forces. The Austrian defeats, and later those of her smaller allies, were explained by a simple equation that one Prussian soldier armed with a Dreyse was three to five times more effective than an Austrian armed with his muzzle-loading Lorenz. As General Franz von Mollinary, one of the unit commanders on the northern front, succinctly expressed it: 'A Prussian company was equivalent to an Austrian battalion.'[6] The potency of such an explanation was enormous, for it allowed the convenient fiction that the army had been defeated by overwhelming odds, and preserved its honour intact. The responsibility for the undeniable mismanagement of the campaign was fixed on Benedek alone, but the inferiority in armaments became the accepted view inside and outside the army as the root cause of the humilation of 1866. With that belief went the conviction, loudly stated, that such a situation must never occur again. Thus the army gladly accepted the myth of the needle-gun in 1866.

The myth still exists, and much more is heard about needle-guns than the other, more pedestrian, merits of the Prussian army.[7] Of course, the true situation was much more complex than Mollinary's attractively simple equation would suggest. The Dreyse was no novelty miracle weapon. It was first introduced in Prussia in 1841,[8] thirteen years before the Austrians rejected it for their own use and adopted the Lorenz. It was a relatively primitive weapon; as William Russell, *The Times* Special Correspondent, remarked after the battle of Königgrätz, it was 'simply a breech-loader of very indifferent quality'. So crude, indeed, were some specimens that Prussian soldiers were unwilling to fire from the shoulder, because the ineffective gas seal allowed burning particles and hot gasses to escape from the breech at the moment of firing. Yet the Dreyse was more effective than the Lorenz — or any muzzle-loader — because it greatly increased the tactical flexibility of the infantry. One Austrian officer who was captured at the battle of Königinhof remarked to Baron Stoffel, the French Military Attache to Berlin,

> 'Our men are demoralised not by the rapidity of fire, for we could find some other way to counterbalance that, but because you [the Prussians] are always ready to fire . . . Our men fear the advantage that quick and easy loading gives you. It is this that demoralises them. In action they feel disarmed the greater part of the time, whereas you are always ready to fire.'[9]

Density of fire in the days of the muzzle-loader meant close formations, and often volley firing. With the breech-loader, the same density and continuity of fire could be achieved with a much looser formation. Austrian tactics were not designed to meet these new circumstances.

The effectiveness of the Dreyse was compounded by the rigidity of the Austrian tactical doctrines. The principles instilled in the army for the conduct of battle were the product of the war of 1859. Then they had lost battles against the French and Piedmontese, despite the fact that the Lorenz was the better infantry arm. The key to the French success was the bayonet charge, often effective against infantry armed with a weapon which was slow or difficult to reload. The success of cold steel against fire power reinforced the existing Austrian penchant for this style of battle, and in the new tactical manual produced in 1862[10] the bayonet charge was preached as the best form of attack, with little or no fire preparation. In the war of 1864 they were successful against the Danes, although some officers did their arithmetic and pointed out how costly in terms of dead and wounded this dashing gallantry had been. If these tactics were wasteful of lives against the Danes, against the Prussians who had precise fire control and the ability to reload quickly, they proved disastrous. The Prussian doctrine emphasised fire power much more strongly and required troops to fight in smaller tactical groups, using cover wherever possible. Burde,[11] who wrote extensively on tactics, described the meeting of the two systems:

'Whenever the Austrians and Prussians met, the former usually attempted a bayonet charge with bravery but the effective fire of the Prussians soon brought the advance to a standstill.' This was certainly Wilczek's experience, and almost all who fought in the north and wrote of their exploits agreed with him. The Austrians, committed to large formal attacks by solid formations in close order, lost more heavily than the Prussians in every battle of the war. Yet this was not simple a matter of the Prussians possessing a better weapon, but the fact that in almost every respect their military machine was superior to that of Austria. The needle-gun was effective because Prussia possessed the means to exploit its advantages; indeed, technologically, by 1866 it was an outdated weapon and the Chassepot (adopted by France in 1867), was a typical 'second generation' needle-gun which corrected many of its faults. But Austria came to believe that the lesson of 1866 was that they had failed to keep in the forefront of technology and innovation. They were mistaken, for the real strength of the Prussian army lay in dusty offices in Berlin, in the 'Rabbit Warren' that housed the General Staff, where logistics and administration had been raised to the level of a serious military science. Paperwork rather than bullets was the fundamental cause of Austria's humiliation.

The nature of this superiority in the war of 1866 has already been well described,[12] but the contest was not between an Austrian army still mentally and spiritually in the age of the battle of Leipzig and the up-to-date Prussian war machine. After the mistakes of 1859 the Austrian army had, ostensibly, been reformed; indeed it was this process of recent renewal which made many observers think that Austria was the more 'modern' force in 1866. The pervasive power of the Imperial Adjutant's office had been curbed, the War Ministry re-established and under Degenfeld a limited programme of reform begun. But in 1859-62, as in the years after Königgrätz, change was inimical to the military system, and was held up or undermined wherever possible. Reform lacked a firm impetus from the highest echelons in the army, who took their tone from the prevailing atmosphere at Court. Franz Joseph's enthusiasm for change waned as his memories of the battlefield of Solferino and his shaming interviews with Napoleon III receded. He accepted limited revisions to the administrative structure, and even a revised tactical doctrine. But he set his face against more radical reforms and, in particular, against any continuing process of change.[13] He believed that the army had failed in 1859 through faulty organisation: the defect was remedied. In 1866, he saw the problem as being connected with a failure in small-arms: an impetus was given to reform in that direction. This policy of piecemeal improvements, tinkering with the system rather than rebuilding it overall, was characteristic of the governmental process, military and civil, of the reign of Franz Joseph.

This 'eternal verity' of the Austrian policy process was quickly realised by all those who wanted to produce effective change. The sanction given to small-arms technologists in 1866-9 to become a kernel of change in a static system was exploited by officers who had no interest in small-arms as such: thus 'reformers' gravitated towards the technological services, like moths to a lantern, because it enabled them to pursue other interests. From the disasters of 1866 grew an elaborate system of innovation within the army, centred on a new section in the War Ministry (the Technical and Military Administrative Committee) which was charged with the thankless task of keeping the army up-to-date.

The contrast between the old approach and the new can be seen in the change of attitude which took place in barely six months at the highest level of the army command. When in the late spring of 1866 some rather halfhearted attempts were made, even as the political situation was worsening, to test new firearms, Archduke Wilhelm (the Inspector-General of Artillery) had a chance exchange with Mollinary,[14] who propounded once again his views on the Danish campaign of 1864 (in which he had fought) and the urgent need for a better firearm. Taxed with the inferiority of Austrian equipment, the Archduke blandly assured him that he could rest content, for *if* it seemed necessary to consider the introduction of a new weapon, then no doubt it would be done. Wilhelm's air of self-satisfaction vanished after the events of June and July. The lackadaisical president of the stillborn Commission of the spring became the active and efficient president of the new Breech-loading Commission of September 1866. The proceedings of this evaluation machinery will be considered below, but the speed of establishment and its rapid (almost too rapid) conclusions and recommendation indicate the profound shock which the system had undergone.

The new small-arms

It was scarcely surprising that one of the first acts after peace was signed at Prague on 23 August 1866 related to breech-loaders, for it was firmly believed that peace with Prussia was likely to be shortlived. For the first time the Emperor issued a direct instruction that a new rifle *was* to be adopted, and urgent steps should be taken to choose the best weapon. A design standard was quickly established for the new rifle and it was determined that Austria should be the first major power in Europe to be equipped with breech-loaders using the novel metallic cartridge. This decision was to be of considerable importance, for it indicated the Austrian intention to be at the forefront of military technology, rather than to adopt an improvement to the more widely favoured needle-gun. The first priority, however, was a system for the conversion of the Lorenz, for which a certain amount of preparatory work had been done during May and June. All the competing designs were to be measured against the basic criteria of low cost and speed and ease of conversion. It was also hoped that some use could be found for the large stocks of paper cartridges used in the Lorenz: some form of needle-gun conversion had earlier seemed likely. Several promising new patterns were submitted by Edward Lindner of New York, and in all, some seventeen designs for needle-guns using paper cartridges were tested. But opinion within the army was moving in favour of metallic cartridges: the Imperial Artillery Committee specified that metallic cartridges had to be used in the new standard rifle, and this principle was eventually extended by the Breech-loading Commission to the designs for the conversion system.

More tests were then made, with fresh designs from Lindner as well as the Snider, which was later adopted in England, the Belgian Albini-Braendlin, the Friedrich and the Prasch systems. But the conversion chosen was that submitted by the Viennese gunsmith Wänzl. It was a simple, if uninspired, transformation: its main advantages were that it was inexpensive and that it was a national design. This psychological factor was important, in the current atmosphere of low morale and disenchantment with the conduct of the army. The Wänzl was put through extensive trials before it was definitely adopted by Imperial command on 8 January 1867. The real matter of interest, however, was the question of the new rifle.

The only conditions for entries in the competition for the new rifle concerned the cartridge and ballistics. These were specified by the Imperial Artillery Committee as calibre 11.15 mm and 1300-1400 feet per second initial velocity. The most important effect of this requirement was to exclude the advanced American repeaters — Henry, Winchester and Spencer — which operated with lower powered cartridges. Despite this, the trials were intended to be conclusive, a complete survey of available arms; nearly 100 different designs were considered at the outset, but only a few were retained for detailed examination. Within the first two weeks, two rifles were clearly outstanding: the American Remington and the Peabody. Both were tested extensively, the Remington being tried for nine days, 20-29 September, and firing over 2,000 shots. After the Peabody was tested, it was decided that the Remington was more efficient and a second series of trials was ordered, with a new sample rifle. This ended on 3 November; on 28 November the Breech-loading Commission gave its final decision, recommending the Remington for provisional adoption and large scale troop trials. Sufficient rifles were ordered for the Twenty-First Jaeger battalion and four infantry battalions to make a complete evaluation.

The Breech-loading Commission had fulfilled its technical brief with the recommendation of the Remington. It was undeniably the best rifle available, but in choosing the American design, dominant political considerations were ignored. The same forces which had worked for the adoption of the Wänzl operated in the question of the new rifle. During December 1866 and January 1867, public opinion was influenced against the Remington. It was claimed, with some justification, that charges for manufacturing rights could be very high, and that a national design should have been chosen. It was also rumoured, more scurrilously, that the Remington rifle was dangerous, that one of them had exploded on trial and injured its user. This particular rumour was so successful that Remington wrote on 3 February 1867 to the President of the Commission, the Archduke Wilhelm, and asked him to refute it. The Archduke replied that: 'No accident had occurred with his rifles on trial, and the Commission was unanimous in the opinion that of all the systems tried up to 28 November 1866, [it] seemed the best . . .'[15] Part of the pressure came from 'patriots', who saw it as a slight on Austrian ingenuity, but commercial motives were a strong and continuing influence. The contract for the army, even if new rifles were made under licence in Austria, would be worth less than for a local product. The arms industry had a clear interest in overthrowing the decision of the Commission. The most powerful element in the Austrian small-arms industry was the Werndl plant at Steyr, and Josef Werndl contracted early in 1867 to convert the majority of the Lorenz muskets to the Wänzl system; it was very likely that he would receive the main production contract for any new rifle. Ostensibly, he had no strong interest in which rifle was adopted for he had not submitted an entry for the breech-loading trials. In fact, from autumn 1866, he was busy promoting a new rifle design by covert means. The specifications of a new arm, designed jointly by Werndl and his factory manager, Karl Holub, were submitted direct to the Minister of War, Baron von John. The War Minister bypassed the arms trials then taking place, and instructed Werndl to prepare a wooden mock-up and a practical working arm. The basic elements of the rifle were not new, and Holub had had them in working form since spring 1866: the decision not to submit them earlier, and through the approved channels, was a deliberate policy on Werndl's part. After the War Minister had approved the project, he delayed handing over a completed 'Werndl-Holub' rifle until after the Breech-loading Commission had chosen the Remington. When the reaction against this decision became effective, their design was the obvious choice for the new Austrian rifle.

It was roughly equivalent to the Remington in most respects, and could fire a little faster. This advantage recommended the rifle to those who saw the Bohemian campaign as the triumph of a quick-firing needle-gun over a slow firing muzzle-loader. The Werndl rifle (Holub's interest in the patents was bought out by Werndl) was put through the same tests as the Remington. It proved to be an effective weapon, if more complicated in design than the Remington, and was officially adopted as the standard issue arm by Imperial command on 28 July 1867. The contract went exclusively to Werndl for producing in all some 611,000 rifles and carbines — the desired end to a somewhat devious political exercise.

The outcome of change

The 1866-7 Breech-loading Commission was only an *entr'acte* in a continuing struggle to secure innovation within the Austrian army, but it also marked a significant point of departure. For the first time, the technologists had been given their head, and used the opportunity to put into practice schemes formulated over the long period of impotence. The Commission selected its personnel from the very best of the available technical officers, and many rose in later years to positions of great eminence and influence.[16] Other alliances were also formed and Josef Werndl encouraged contacts between his designers and the military technologists. Even stronger ties were forged, Werndl again leading the way by marrying his daughters to promising artillery officers. But beyond these specifics, the successful conclusion of the Commission's work marked a more general shift of attitudes. The effect of the war of 1866 had been to alter the status of the argument about innovation, from *whether* technological advance was necessary to questions as to *how much* progress was desirable. After the war even the reactionary elements in the army could no longer disregard the basic mechanics of warfare: once the logic of the needle-gun was accepted, the argument that the army should institutionalise the search for progress was greatly reinforced. Thus what had seemed before 1866 a visionary programme for a centre of research within the army was now possible.

But despite this propensity to change, the creation of a new institution posed great difficulties. What scope was it to have, what range of responsibilities, and most important of all, to whom would it be responsible? For the crux of a new institution, if it was to be effective, was that it would alter the balance of power and authority within the army. It is at this point that the scope of this article can be broadened beyond the detailed specifics of technology, for innovation was now a central political issue, a pawn in the battle for authority and jurisdiction.

After the war of 1866, the centre of the military stage in Austria was occupied by the Archduke Albrecht, the conqueror of the Italians at Custozza, and the dynasty's most successful soldier since his father, Karl. In September 1866, he was appointed the *Armeeoberkommandant*, which gave him substantial powers over most aspects of military activity, but especially over future policy and planning. It was an *ad hominem* appointment, in recognition of his unique position within the army: administratively it was a recipe for certain conflict. The post-war period was the moment to push through reform, of which the small-arms question was one aspect. Albrecht, although he accepted certain areas of change as being necessary, was violently opposed to radical reform. His views were succinctly stated in a pamphlet entitled *Concerning Responsibility in War*. He made it clear that war was a matter of morale, not material, and that what was truly important was the inner unity of the army and a fostering of the 'old Austrian soldier spirit'.[17] His views dominated the unfortunate Minister of War, von John, and the progress of reform in the first year after the war was slow. In January 1868, von John was succeeded by Franz von Kuhn, a soldier of avowedly advanced opinions and an energetic reformer. He did not hesitate to attack the position of the Archduke head on. He made it clear that power in the army must pass through properly constituted administrative channels, and the fact that the Archduke would undoubtedly command the army in war should not provide him with *carte blanche* for engrossing all power in his hands.

In the two years after Königgrätz, two attitudes had evolved towards reform. The first, exemplified by Albrecht, accepted a minimal programme of change, repeating the pattern of the post-1859 period. The other view, which now found its most powerful advocate in the new War Minister, argued that if the army was to remain comparable with the other armies of Europe, and, more important, be capable of defeating the Prussians when the need arose, radical alterations were necessary. To this the first group responded that this would shatter the unity of the army and render it weaker than before, to which the radicals riposted that drastic change was Austria's only hope. These groupings extended only to professional matters: on wider political issues, such as the effects of the new constitutional arrangements with Hungary, the army spoke with a united voice. The crucial battles in the campaign for ultimate authority within the army were fought over the creation of the new centre for research.

The two parties hardened on this issue because it was clear that whichever was victorious would swing the balance of power decidedly in its favour. Albrecht wanted to preserve his prerogatives over development and planning and to set up a vague supervisory body to co-ordinate the work of the existing (and largely ineffectual) Artillery and Engineer Committees. Kuhn proposed a much more active body which would oversee the whole body of military science, and would proffer unified solutions to the problem of modern warfare. It was to be charged with a direct responsibility to investigate work in other countries, to test new developments, and examine on a continuing basis the equipment and procedures of the Austrian army in the light of up-to-date experience. It was to be headed by an eminent and distinguished officer, and would make its recommendations directly to the War Minister, rather than to any intervening official. Clearly, by these means, he intended to preempt many of the decisions which Albrecht considered pertained to his position. The plans for the Committee were the subject of almost a year's debate, with the Emperor acting as the recipient of appeals from both parties. When the issue was resolved with the creation of the Technical and Administrative Military Committee at the end of June 1869, it was obvious that a modified version of Kuhn's programme had been accepted. The first President of the Committee was Arthur Graf Bylandt-Rheidt, the former President of the Artillery Committee, and a veteran of the breech-loader trials. With him went many of the most active and intelligent young technical officers. At the end of April 1869, Albrecht had grudgingly exchanged his position as Army Commander-in-Chief for that of General Inspector of the Army, and it seemed that the reformers had won a substantial victory.

Inevitably the struggle for power within the army did not end there. Despite Kuhn's efforts to build a secure institutional bulwark for the supremacy of the War Ministry, he remained embattled until his resignation was forced in 1874. Thereafter, although Albrecht did not recover his former powers, his capacity to frustrate and delay was much enhanced, and he became more and more a totem for those with a traditional concept of the army. The Technical and Administrative Military Committee survived even beyond the end of the Monarchy in 1918, but its position was only as strong as its master, the War Minister, cared to make it. Its apogee was probably in the period 1876-88, when its President, Arthur Bylandt-Rheidt, served as War Minister. But his successors on the Committee had neither his experience and prestige, nor his political skill, and as successive war ministers displayed a manifest lack of interest in technical matters, the institution languished, an object lesson as to how, within a bureacracy, power is rarely static. On one level it was entirely successful. Its routines and methods of operation made it highly efficient, and commentators from other armies, if they criticised the Austrians in general, were usually quick to point out the excellence of their research and technical services. Their committee's journal, *Mitteilungen über Gegenstande des Artillerie and Geniewesens*, rapidly achieved international renown. But as the Committee was progressively starved of funds, its practical impact declined. The 1869 scheme which envisaged the Committee as the intellectual forcing house of the army, operating to maintain high standards in every technical field, and turning out graduates to carry the gospel back to the regiments, was largely frustrated. Where Kuhn had wanted a 'school of the army', it became much more a research institute which was increasingly cut off from the realities of military life.

But despite the comparative failure of the attempt to modernise the army, which had been Kuhn's prime objective, the issue of innovation remained significant. When Conrad tried from his vantage point of Chief of the General Staff to do what Kuhn had tried to do as War Minister, both the issues and the political manoeuvres had a marked similarity. Within the army, the balance of power had altered during the 1890s in favour of the Chief of Staff, who secured a role independent of the Ministry of War, and on his appointment in 1906 as a replacement for the aged Beck, Conrad sought as Kuhn had done to strengthen his position by extending his sphere of activity. His conflicts with the Emperor over 'intrusions' into areas of policy beyond his competence became common knowledge, but the basic issue which caused the army to polarise was once again innovation and reform.[18] Conrad, as protégé of the Archduke Franz Ferdinand, the Heir Presumptive, enjoyed his backing for the programme of change, which gave it the sustained support lacking in Kuhn's attempts of forty years before. As a result, the programme of change was much wider in its scope, an attempt, albeit only partly successful, at a root-and-branch transformation. Clearly, these parallels have their limitations but the attitudes expressed by those who opposed radical change had altered little over the years. For them, change beyond the necessary minimum remained a fundamental threat to the established principles on which the army operated.

Were a phrase needed to describe this attitude, it would be difficult to better Musil's remark in *A Man Without Qualities*: 'There in Kakania, that misunderstood State that has since vanished, which was in so many things a model (though all unacknowledged), there was speed, too, of course; but not too much speed.'[19] It is paradoxical that nineteenth-century armies, which by reason of their institutional coherence and longevity, reacted so strongly against change, were also the institutions most steadily subjected to the pressures of change. Advances in technology and the art of war meant that the *status quo* could never be fully restored; that no sooner was one change embraced than a new development demanded attention. In this sense, technology is a touchstone, though one of limited value, whereby military attitudes can be judged. One may ask whether technological change was resisted: often it was, and the reasons for this resistance are (usually) fairly clear. But it is more profitable to ask what *kinds* of innovation were *particularly* resisted, and why. Given the answers to these questions about the great armies of Europe, our understanding of the collective 'military mind' (if such a thing exists) would be greatly enriched.

Notes

1. J. Steinberg, *Yesterday's Deterrent*, London, 1965, p. 199.
2. See C. H. Roads, *The British Soldier's Firearm*, London, 1964, p. 294.
3. See, for example, the works of Von Bernhardi and Erskine Childers, *War and the Arme Blanche*. The Austrians, after 1884, abolished the lance even for lancer regiments, on the assumption that the future role of cavalry in war would be scouting and reconnaissance.
4. Germany was particularly prone to the use of this device. See G. Craig, 'Chancellor and Chief of Staff in the Second German Empire', in *War, Politics and Diplomacy*, London, 1966, p. 124.
5. See Count Wilczek, *Happy Retrospect*, London, 1934, p. 59.
6. A. von Mollinary, *46 Ans dans l'armee Austro-Hongroise, 1833-79*, Paris, 1913, Vol. II, p. 121.
7. This is especially common in popular accounts. See E. Crankshaw, *The Habsburgs*, London, 1971, p. 244: 'Königgrätz was above all decided by the superiority of the Prussian needle-gun, the new breech-loading quick-firing rifle, used for the first time in a major war.'
8. In 1833, 1,100 rifles were issued to the Fusiliers for testing, and many improvements were made to correct inadequacies shown up. In October 1841 the first production order for 60,000 rifles was issued, and by 1849, 288,000 had been distributed. The main Prussian infantry arm at Königgrätz was not the M 1841, but the later development, the M 1862.
9. See Colonel Baron Stoffel, *Military Reports addressed to the French War Minister 1866-70*, translated R. Home, London, 1872, p. 64. See also pp. 4-5 for a perceptive analysis of the influence of the needle-gun on the war.
10. See *Exercier Reglement für die K. K. Fusstruppen*, Vienna, 1862.
11. See J. Burde, *Problems in Applied Tactics*, English translation, London, 1894.
12. Incomparably the best modern account is G. Craig, *The Battle of Königgrätz*, London, 1965.
13. He refused repeated attempts by generals Gablenz and Schönfeld after the war of 1864 to carry out a thorough analysis of the war, and snubbed a more junior officer who made the same appeal. See E. Glaise Horstenau, *Franz Joseph's Weggefährte*, Vienna, 1930.
14. See Mollinary, *op. cit.*, Vol. II, p. 103.
15. See *Engineering*, 9 November 1866, and F. Silas (tr.), *Le Fusil Remington: rapport officiel sur les essais faits à Vienna pour le K K Hinterladungs Gewehr Commission*, Vienna, 1867.
16. Perhaps the most noteworthy example was Alfred von Kropatschek, who rose to become Inspector-General of the Artillery. Kropatschek invented the first successful European magazine rifle, adopted by France and Portugal, as well as a revolver for Austria, and many other designs.
17. *Uber Verantwortlichkeit im Kriege*. See 'Erzherzog Albrecht und das Altösterreichische Soldatengeist' in H. v. Srbik, *Aus Osterreichs Vergangenheit*, Vienna, 1949. See also Albrecht's pamphlet, *Wie soll Osterreichs Heer organisiert sein*.
18. For the technological progress of the Austro-Hungarian Army under Conrad see Rudolf Kizling, 'Die Entwicklung des österreichisch – ungarischen Wehrmacht seit der Annexionskrise, 1908', *Berliner Monatshefte*, 1934.
19. Robert Musil, *A Man Without Qualities*, English translation, London, 1953, Vol. I, p. 65.

PART 2

As the role of military institutions within society increased in importance, analysts began to look for the effects which this interpenetration had on society at large. Part 2 of this book is concerned with the effects of this growing dominance of society by its defenders. Volker Berghahn looks at what is now the classic case of society turned towards military objectives, and he shows how the subtle and complex calculations which underpinned the German naval programme broke down in the last years before the First World War. Clive Trebilcock looks at the positive effects which military expenditure exerted on national economies and societies, effects which have until now largely been clouded by anti-militarist propaganda. Norman Stone writes of the problems of organising a national economy to accommodate the differing demands of wartime and peacetime armies. Geoffrey Best considers the way ideas of how war should be fought modified under the pressure of changing circumstance, how indeed the old separation between soldier and civilian became blurred. Indeed by the end of the period covered by this book, the age of total mobilisation for the war effort was upon us. In a sense this second part of the book reinforces the conclusions of the first, that military institutions are separate from the societies which surround them, and between the two a growing gap of misunderstanding and incomprehension yawned.

5 NAVAL ARMAMENTS AND SOCIAL CRISIS: GERMANY BEFORE 1914[1]

Volker Berghahn

The construction of the German battle fleet under Alfred von Tirpitz during the two decades before the First World War has occupied a central place in historical writing on modern Germany since 1918. This interest in the causes and effects of Wilhelmine naval policy is not surprising in view of the widespread feeling that Tirpitz's battle fleet contributed, perhaps more than any other factor, to the heightening of international tensions that ended in war in August 1914. Inevitably the historical debate led to many differences of opinion which were most marked during the interwar period and which continued even after 1945.[2] But historians, it appears, now agree on at least one point: the expansion of the Imperial Navy under Tirpitz cannot be satisfactorily tackled with the methodology of traditional military history. Although the discussion of the military-strategic aspects of our problem is continuing,[3] the Kaiser's fleet was most decidedly not just a technical toy or a military juggernaut conceived in a vacuum removed from political and social conditions in the Reich. On the contrary, the leadership of Germany set great political hopes on naval armaments and saw in them a vehicle for solving the manifold internal and external problems with which the Prusso-German monarchy was confronted at the turn of the century. This means that an analysis of Tirpitz's naval policy cannot do without the tools of modern social history. Those who refuse to apply these tools will not be able to understand its true and truly staggering dimensions. It is the great merit of Eckart Kehr to have been the first to grasp this point.[4] But unfortunately a whole generation of German historians chose to ignore his findings so that it took more than thirty years for his contribution to be appreciated.[5]

What were the great internal and external problems which naval armaments were supposed to help to solve? As far as the domestic aspect is concerned, the expansion of the Imperial Navy must be seen in the context of the growing structural crisis of the Prusso-German constitutional and social system. A first impression of the nature of this crisis can be gained by referring to the Reich Constitution of 1871. A cursory glance at this document will show that powers were very unevenly distributed among the various organs and that the constitutional rights of the Crown surpassed by far those of the Reichstag, the popular assembly, and of the Bundesrat, the representation of the federal princes. Without going into details, it can be said that, taken together, the privileges of the monarch amounted to giving him a quasi-absolutist position. Certainly the limited powers of the Reichstag compared very unfavourably with the concentration of constitutional rights in the hands of the Kaiser and his fellow princes. The popular assembly lacked the classic attributes of a parliamentary system, except for embryonic budgetary powers, and, although its deputies were elected by universal manhood suffrage, it was but marginally involved in the decision making process. Liberals who were unhappy with this constitutional arrangement were left with a faint hope that reforms might result in a gradual expansion of parliamentary powers and that the Reich would in the long run develop along British lines. But Imperial Germany had a long way to go before a Westminster-type political system could be established.

This impression will be reinforced if one cares to look at the constitutions of the German federal states with their elaborate class franchise and at the *Realverfassung*, the *de facto* distribution of power. Again careful analysis will show that a small circle of men wielded an excess of political and social influence so that Wilhelm Liebknecht was not exaggerating when he stated after the founding of the Reich that Germany was, at heart, 'a princely insurance company against democracy'. This small 'strategic clique',[6] whose policies in the 1890s have been examined more recently by John Röhl,[7] was supported by a conservative bureaucracy and a military establishment which, practically exempt from parliamentary control, was almost exclusively in the hands of the Kaiser while maintaining intimate social and political ties with the landed aristocracy.[8] As is well known, the connection between the military and civilian authorities on the one hand and the agrarians on the other was particularly strong in Prussia, the largest and most powerful federal state. Whatever one's approach, the analysis of the constitutional and political realities in the Second Empire invariably lead to the conclusion that this state in the heart of Europe was essentially an autocracy.

But what is perhaps even more important for an understanding of the domestic problems of Wilhelmine Germany is that the Crown and the forces supporting it made strenuous attempts to secure the survival of this old fashioned political system in the twentieth century. They had come to appreciate the great value of the existing constitutional order as a means of securing and preserving economic and social privileges at a time when the share of agriculture in the production of the empire's wealth was in fact declining. In the final analysis this decline was due to the growth of an industrial economy which had gradually come to supersede the hitherto predominantly agrarian economy. This process was accelerated by an economic depression which struck the grain growing East Elbian Junkers from the mid-1870s onwards.[9] Prices for agricultural produce declined, leading to the relative impoverishment of the landed aristocracy. Their reaction to this development is well summed up by the Conservative Reichstag deputy and East Prussian landowner Elard von Oldenburg-Januschau who exclaimed in April 1904:[10] 'Being poor is no misfortune, but falling into poverty is one.' Yet impoverishment was not just a personal tragedy. For, as Oldenburg put it, 'every mortgage taken out on a piece of land [as a result of] sheer need will erode the foundations on which the Kaiser's crown is resting. The security of the crown is rooted in the desire of innumerable lesser crown-bearers to hand on their little empires to their descendants.' Alfred von Waldersee had visions of similar consequences which threatened to follow from the relative decline of the landed aristocracy and which were exacerbated by the growing wealth of the new commercial bourgeoisie.[11] This social group was making great fortunes in trade and industry and began to compete with the life style of the Junkers, many of whom lived in splendid stately homes but were so poor that their 'daughters frequently had to make their own court dress'.[12] 'In the Old Prussian provinces', Waldersee noted in his diary, 'a large scale exchange of landed property is taking place before our eyes. New owners of considerably inferior quality replace the old ones. The genuinely conservative elements of Prussia are being destroyed and a good deal of monarchical loyalty is being lost.'[13]

In view of such developments it is not surprising that the agrarians should try to use their powerful position within the political system to block such undesirable tendencies. But it is equally plausible that those social groups which were emerging in the wake of Germany's industrial revolution, especially the working classes, could see little benefit in the rigid preservation of a preindustrial social and political order. They demanded the establishment of a parliamentary democracy through which they would be able to participate in the decision making processes of the Reich. Domestically, therefore, Germany saw herself exposed to an increasing pressure 'from below' which, in turn, generated a profound fear of change among the ruling caste. And since the industrialisation of the country continued at a rapid pace, it was a spiral without end: the potential of those who were dissatisfied with the *status quo* grew larger and reinforced, in turn, existing anxieties among the conservative groups. It was clear that something had to be done to stop this process — something that would *contain* the threat 'from below'.

The most radical countermeasure which was never far from the Kaiser and his advisers was to stage a *Staatsstreich*, i.e. a violent *coup* against the Reichstag and the working class movement with the aim of revising the Reich Constitution in a backward direction and of re-establishing preconstitutional conditions.[14] This policy required a military instrument which was completely loyal to the Crown, and this became the main function of the Army which acted as a covert deterrent against left-wing movements or, failing that, was to serve as the last bastion for the preservation of the monarchy. That the Kaiser and his advisers were quite prepared to use the army for this purpose was again made clear in the mid-1890s when the Reich appeared to be slithering into a major confrontation between the Crown and the parliamentary forces. Worried about the erosion of the monarchical position, military and court circles began to push for a preventive strike against the uncooperative Reichstag and the growing Social Democratic Party (SPD) as a means of solving the permanent constitutional dilemma. 'In view of the trememdous growth of the Social Democrat movement', General Waldersee wrote in a memorandum to the Kaiser,

> 'it appears to me to be inevitable that we are approaching the moment when the state's instruments of power must measure themselves with those of the working masses . . . But if the struggle is inevitable . . . the state cannot gain anything from postponing it . . . I feel that it is in the state's interest not to leave it to the Social Democrat leaders to decide when the great reckoning is to begin; rather it should do everything possible to force an early decision. For the moment, the state is, with certainty, still strong enough to suppress any rising.'[15]

But Reich Chancellor Clodwig von Hohenlohe-Schillingsfürst and the Prussian State Ministry were not happy about these proposals, fearing that a collision course would weaken the position of the Crown instead of strengthening it. Hohenlohe therefore pursued a different strategy which preconditioned a 'calming of public opinion which is afraid of a reactionary policy'.[16] Only when 'the fear of the socialists exceeds anxieties about a reactionary policy', as the Baden Ambassador paraphrased Hohenlohe's arguments, 'of which one expects the abolition of civil liberties', elections to the Reichstag would once more return government-loyal majorities and this, in turn, would lead to a general 'improvement of the overall political situation'. In other words, the Reich Chancellor envisaged a rallying (*Sammlung*) of those forces in German society which were frightened by the growth of the allegedly 'revolutionary' SPD. But he and his advisers were still looking for a vehicle to bring this about. The traditional means of the Bismarckian period — anti-socialism and protectionism — had, by this time, become too blunted to entice the agrarians and the bourgeoisie into an alliance on the basis of the *status quo*. Johannes von Miquel, the Prussian Minister of Finance and a representative of the Bismarckian generation, tried it, but failed with his particular concept of *Sammlung* to attract those elements in the Reichstag on whose support the government was dependent for the smooth implementation of its legislation under the changed parliamentary conditions of the late 1890s.[17]

This more powerful interest aggregate was at last found and activated in the shape of an ambitious armaments programme after which the rumours of an impending *Staatsstreich* subsided very quickly. This is not the place to recount how naval expansion helped, at the turn of the century, to weld the agrarians and the bourgeoisie together against the left and to distract people from the inadequacies and inequalities of the monarchical system.[18] The various studies which are by now available on this subject show, beyond reasonable doubt, that the building of the German battle fleet was stimulated primarily by political and economic considerations and initiated a period of Wilhelmine history which, by comparison with the crisis of the mid-1890s, was relatively stable and peaceful.[19] Although it did not last for more than a few years, it nevertheless inspired fresh optimism in the viability of the Prusso-German political system.

The compromise between the agrarians and the middle classes which is of basic importance to an understanding of the subsequent development of the empire implied that the conservatives voted for naval armaments which the bourgeoisie regarded as the indispensable foundation of a future German world position. In return for this, the agrarians gained the support of the middle class parties for increased agricultural tariffs on which the former insisted as a safeguard against rapid economic decline.[20] Through their cooperation both groups, moreover, hoped to curb the growth of socialism, though less by means of outright repression than by appealing to the patriotism and material interest of the working classes.[21] 'We do not wage our struggle against the Social Democrats', Reich Chancellor Bernhard von Bülow declared, 'in order to hit the worker, but in order to pull him away from the ensnarements of the socialists and to accustom him to the monarchical order.'[22] The idea of a powerful navy with the emotional and economic benefits to be derived from it, so Tirpitz and his followers believed, possessed the strength 'to revive the patriotic spirit of all classes and to fill them with love for Kaiser and Reich'.[23] To secure markets for German industry, to preserve agrarian privileges, to avoid a social revolution by means of full employment and a nationalist ideology with the Kaiser acting as the focus of a successful Bonapartist government — those, in short, were the ambitious aims of the 'heirs of Bismarck'[24] who were faced with having to operate a highly inflexible political system at a time of rapid social and economic change.

It is in this broader context that we must also see another idea which Tirpitz developed in connection with his armaments programme, namely the idea of destroying the embryonic budgetary powers of the popular assembly. This objective seemed all the more desirable since it was to be expected that universal suffrage might some day result in a more persistent anti-government majority in the Reichstag. Unless the navy was, like the army, removed from the possibility of parliamentary interference, William II might suddenly find himself in difficulties similar to those faced by his grandfather in the 1860s. At that time the majority in the Prussian Diet had opposed the plans which the king had with regard to the army.[25] Might a future Reichstag, composed of oppositional deputies, not try to do the same when the monarch was just about to use 'his' navy has a lever against other sea powers? Clearly, in order to prevent this from happening the navy had to be withdrawn to an extra-constitutional position in which the monarch could dispose of the organisation, size and use of the fleet as he alone saw fit.

In designing his naval programme, Tirpitz therefore also set out to establish an Iron Budget (*Marineaeternat*), and the way to achieve this was by introducing bills which provided for a certain number of capital ships as well as their automatic replacement after twenty years. Once this had been approved by the present Reichstag, a future more left-wing assembly was, constitutionally, no longer in a position to reduce the naval establishment by refusing to approve the naval estimates. It was an ingenious plan which would have effectively prevented the Imperial Navy from becoming a 'parliamentary fleet' like the Royal Navy. In the final analysis, the whole concept of a navy under the exclusive command of the Kaiser is yet another manifestation of the keen desire of William II and his advisers to maintain and, where possible, strengthen the existing quasi-absolutist political system against parliamentary currents in German society.[26]

It has been mentioned at the beginning of this article that the decision to increase naval armaments was not only influenced by internal considerations. The widespread optimism about Germany's splendid future among the great powers notwithstanding, the international position of the Reich was as precarious as the domestic one. At least there existed strong fears concerning the development of the international system which led the Reich government to look for potential remedies. Many people — businessmen as well as publicists — were worried by the possibility of compact empires emerging in the future which were protected against foreign competition by high tariff walls. It appears that this fear was, to a large extent, generated by the experience of the Great Depression of the 1870s and 1880s which had seen the decline of Free Trade and the adoption of protectionist policies by all major powers.[27] Many German observers expected this process to continue, ending in the creation of large power blocs which competed for the resources and markets of the globe. They now asked the anxious question as to what would, in these circumstances, happen to Germany, who experienced fast industrial growth at home, but which, by the turn of the century, had acquired but a small overseas empire. Evidently she was dependent on the goodwill of the other colonial powers, and if they decided, for whatever reason, to close their doors to German goods, German industrial prosperity was vitally threatened.

There appeared to be only one alternative to this: Germany had to try to gain belatedly a colonial empire commensurate with her economic power, even though the 'scramble' for formal empires was largely over. But just because the globe had already been carved up between other nations, German ambitions to achieve a strong position among the major world powers were forced to take a detour: the Reich, it was argued, required a navy which was employable as a political and, if necessary, even as a military lever against other countries. Since the latter were not expected to cede their colonial possessions voluntarily, they had to be bullied into surrendering them. And even if some weaker nations – Portugal, for example – might have been prepared to cooperate with the Germans, there remained always the first sea power, Great Britain, to be dealt with, without whose approval the Germans would never be able to make colonial conquests. This meant, of course, that the naval lever was effective only if it could also be used against the British power position. As long as this condition remained unfulfilled, German aspirations were always threatened by the direct or indirect intervention of Britain. Ultimately, the Imperial Navy had to be strong enough to be able to ignore or over-rule a British veto.

Tirpitz believed that he could build such a fleet. If the German navy could be increased to two thirds of the British strength in the home waters, the Reich, so Tirpitz told the Kaiser in September 1899, would be in a position to conduct a 'great overseas policy'.[28] When reaching this crucial 2:3 ratio, the German battle fleet would, he thought, gain a genuine chance of victory in the event of a British attack. Should the British government, on the other hand, decide against an aggressive policy, the sheer weight of naval power right on Britain's doorstep, so Tirpitz reckoned, would persuade her to tolerate, or even actively support, German colonial claims. These may seem to be megalomaniac calculations. That they were nevertheless entertained in the Reich Navy Office emerges, *inter alia*, from the following file note of February 1900 which asserted:

> 'that the enlargement of the British fleet cannot proceed at the same rate as ours because the size of their fleet requires a considerably larger number of replacements. The [attached] table demonstrates ... that England ... will have to construct and replace a fleet almost three times as large as the German one envisaged by the [projected]

Navy Law [of 1900] if she expects to have an efficient fleet . . . in 1920. The inferiority in tonnage which our battle fleet will continue to have *vis-à-vis* Britain in 1920 shall be compensated for by a particularly good training of our personnel and better tactical manoeuvrability of large battle formations [*in der taktischen Schulung im grossen Verbande*] . . . The [enclosed] figures . . . on the tonnage which both battle fleets keep in service amount to a superiority of Germany. In view of the notorious difficulties in England to recruit enough personnel, it is unlikely that this favourable position will change.'[29]

A few weeks earlier Tirpitz had written that, after the completion of the naval programme, 'we shall no doubt have a good chance even *vis-à-vis* England owing to [our] geographical position, system of military service, mobilisation, torpedo boats, tactical training, systematic organisational build-up [and] unified command by the monarch'.[30] For, indeed, 'without a victorious battle' the Royal Navy would always be in a position to cut Germany off from other continents.[31] 'Everything depends on [the word] victorious. Hence let us concentrate on this victory.' After all, Tirpitz concluded his remarks, one could not really carve up 'the bear's skin before the bear has been killed'.

Other authors have subjected these calculations of Tirpitz and his advisers to a harsh strategical critique and pinpointed the manifold flaws in his political thinking.[32] But in order to do this competently, the historian must first try to find out precisely what the German plans consisted of. The new documents which became available to research during the 1960s show that Tirpitz pursued nothing less than the objectives which have been outlined above. He embarked upon an armaments programme, to be completed by 1920, which, if executed as planned, would have helped to stabilise the precarious domestic situation and open up to the Prusso-German monarchy a secure place among the great powers of the world. On the other hand, if the original calculations were proven wrong, the disintegration of the ambitious naval programme which occupied a key position in government policy planning after 1898 would be bound to have far-reaching repercussions on the political system as a whole. The latent crisis of German society which the expansion of the fleet with its domestic and external advantages was supposed to resolve for good would then come to the surface and create a most dangerous political situation.

It cannot be said that Tirpitz was naïvely unaware of these problems and dangers. In fact, it is for this reason that, to begin with, he surrounded his programme with a veil of the utmost secrecy. He was understandably very concerned not to alarm the British unduly and, above all, prematurely. Nor did he wish to arouse the opposition of the

Reichstag deputies on whose goodwill and cooperation he remained dependent as long as the Iron Budget had not been achieved and who were always worried about the financial burden of armaments. The most important weapon in his concern for secrecy was the idea of expanding the fleet in stages.[33] Tirpitz planned to add only so many ships to the navy as the domestic and diplomatic constellations permitted. The various fleet bills were not introduced on the spur of the moment, but were projected years in advance, essentially since the turn of the century. Tirpitz merely waited for the most propitious moment to introduce them.

Now that the archives have been fully opened, there can be little doubt that such a *Stufenplan* was developed by Tirpitz and his advisers despite the fact that it put all other government policies, whether financial, diplomatic or social, into a tight straitjacket. They were military men with a firm political vision and an almost fanatical belief in systematic, step-by-step procedure. They realised that German policy would pass through a 'danger zone', but they were undeterred by the political difficulties that lay ahead.[34] For they wanted to build a navy which would help to overcome the cleavages in German society and initiate a new era of domestic peace for the class ridden Wilhelmine monarchy; they were projecting a battle fleet which, put under the exclusive command of the Kaiser, would, in the age of twentieth century imperialism, be available as a political and military lever against Britain in order to secure for the Reich a world position, bringing peace and prosperity to all classes and obviating the need for domestic reform. It was Tirpitz himself who put these calculations into a nutshell when he wrote as early as 1895:

> 'In my view Germany will, in the coming century, rapidly drop from her position as a great power unless we begin to develop our maritime interests energetically, systematically and without delay, to no small degree also because this great patriotic task and the economic benefits to be derived from it will offer a strong palliative against educated and uneducated Social Democrats.'[35]

This is the dual sense, i.e. directly as well as indirectly via a tough foreign policy, in which Tirpitz's plan has been defined as an 'innerpolitical crisis strategy'.[36] For a number of years — roughly between 1898 and 1904 — this crisis strategy appeared to be working fairly well.[37] The domestic and diplomatic calculations on which the naval programme was based seemed to be realistic and reasonably well founded. But by 1904 Britain had definitely become alerted to the danger that was growing up on the other side of the North Sea. In the diplomatic field, the turn in British policy found its first and indirect expression in the creation of the Entente Cordiale; in the field of naval policy, Britain's reaction culminated in the decision to engage the Reich in an open arms race.

This arms race began as a quantitative one which did not worry Tirpitz too much. As has been seen, the Reich Navy Office believed that numerically the Imperial Navy would even be able to catch up with the Royal Navy. But soon a qualitative dimension was added to this quantitative arms race and it was this dual character of the Anglo-German arms race that upset Tirpitz's original plan. The German calculations of the turn of the century were called into question when the Admiralty decided to build the 'Dreadnought', i.e. a type of capital ship which was markedly superior to the ships envisaged under Tirpitz's long term numerical expansion. If we want to gain a fuller understanding of the reasons for the disaster which struck the Imperial Navy from 1905 onwards, we must turn to the financial side of the armaments programme. Tirpitz had designed his plan in such a way that it could be financed without tax increases out of the Reich's revenue. In fact, the need to circumnavigate the thorny tax issue was another reason why the Reich Navy Office adopted the idea of an expansion by stages. The various Navy Laws were supposed to be adjusted to the expected further growth of the German economy and the increased revenue which the Reich would automatically obtain from it. In accordance with this consideration, Tirpitz had presented the Reichstag with estimates which covered several years and to which he promised to adhere. Until about 1905, the Navy Secretary did, in fact, succeed in keeping more or less within the financial limits set by the Navy Laws although he managed to do so only by blatantly disregarding those needs of the navy which were not directly contributing to his first priority, the numerical increase in capital ships.[38]

However, with the British decision to build dreadnoughts, the costs of the individual battleship rose so steeply that Tirpitz's funds were eaten up by qualitative improvements. For he now had not only to construct the projected *number* of ships, but also to increase their fighting power, if the Imperial Navy was ever to become the power-political lever against Britain it was intended to be. It was evidently futile trying to reach a numerical 2:3 ratio, if at the same time the German ships were decisively inferior to the British as regards armour, speed and firing power. The dual pressure of a quantitative and qualitative arms race threw the German programme between the millstones of international and domestic politics. It raised the dangerous issue of higher taxes which was bound to divide those parties which had hitherto supported the broad aims of Tirpitz's naval and world policy. With the arms race accelerating, it became therefore increasingly unlikely that the German battle fleet would ever be able to fulfil the stabilising function assigned to it at the turn of the century.

It must be emphasised that the disintegration of Tirpitz's grand design was a gradual process and that he did his best to arrest it. But all he could do was to retard the final collapse of his life work while his demagogic propaganda and his political trickery merely fostered the growing opposition to his ambitious programme. Instead of uniting the parties and augmenting the external might of the Reich, naval armaments became a divisive force which contributed to the diplomatic isolation of Germany, and did so perhaps even more decisively than the spectacular manoeuvres of the German Foreign Office during the Moroccan crisis.

Any serious attempt to arrive at a realistic assessment of the domestic and international situation ought to have shown Tirpitz that he could not win a quantitative as well as a qualitative arms race against Britain and that the appearance of the dreadnoughts was the beginning of the end of his grand design. Of course, this would have required a very sober estimate of the economic potential of the two antagonists and a subtle appreciation of the British determination to resist the German challenge which few people in Germany possessed. But it cannot be said that the Reich government blindly stumbled into the subsequent disaster. Thus Albert Ballin, the Director-General of the Hamburg-Amerika-Linie, warned Bülow in July 1908:[39] 'We cannot possibly engage ourselves in an arms race in dreadnoughts against the much wealthier British.' It is interesting that this was the verdict of a calculating businessman who knew Britain well, while the men round the Kaiser, many of whom approached politics with crude military categories, had little understanding of the importance of economic factors in international relations. Indeed, a ruling elite whose world of ideas was steeped in precapitalist values and which considered the British parliamentary system weak and corrupt could hardly be expected to arrive at an accurate view of the situation. The German 'heroes' flatly underestimated the political system across the North Sea and never understood the despised 'shopkeepers'.[40]

But what made the miscalculations of the respective arms race potentials even worse was the emergence in Germany of an encirclement mentality. In assessing the importance of this factor, it is important to remember that, objectively, Germany had caused her own isolation when she embarked upon her dangerous naval and world policy. However, these facts were soon forgotten inside the Reich and armaments now appeared to be a response to, rather than a cause of, containment. At first this reversal of cause and effect had obvious domestic advantages. By appealing to the fear of encirclement, the Reich government was able to mobilise defensive instincts in the population which helped to counteract the centrifugal forces in German society which were developing over the financial issue. But the excessive exploitation of this fear introduced an element of irrationalism into German politics which slowly but surely also began to affect the Kaiser and his advisers. They, too, became incapable of differentiating between cause and effect and of making their decisions on the basis of a full and rational examination of political reality. The encirclement hysteria was contagious and resulted in a self-imprisonment.[41] A glance at the Kaiser's marginal comments or at the German press will support the impression that many Germans, and especially the ruling groups, began to live in a world in which the facts counted for less than the wild fictions about the opponent and his aims. This means that the whole encirclement phenomenon has to be tackled with socio-psychological categories.[42] They are most likely to shed new light on the curious behaviour of the Wilhelmine elites before 1914 and on why so many of their policies were based on 'illusions'[43] which, because they were pursued with such great dogmatism, merely made things worse.

The trouble which Tirpitz's plans had run into by 1908 can be gauged from the new Navy Law (*Novelle*) which he introduced during that year. Only two years earlier, the Navy Secretary had successfully completed the third stage of his long term programme. The Reichstag approved six capital ships, thus extending the regular building tempo of the period 1898-1905 up to 1912. Apart from this numerical increase which brought the navy closer to the Iron Budget, the 1906 bill also provided for qualitative improvements, i.e. the building of German dreadnoughts. The German public and the Reich Navy Office expected the financial appropriations for this bill to last until 1912. Then Tirpitz hoped to get a final bill accepted which would establish the Iron Budget of sixty capital ships to be replaced every twenty years. But by 1907 it was clear that the Admiralty would continue to increase the displacement of the British capital ships, and since Tirpitz was still not prepared to drop out of the arms race, he was forced to follow suit. This pressure to use the money, appropriated in 1906, for the construction of 'improved dreadnoughts' meant, of course, that the funds which were supposed to last until 1911 could be expected to be eaten up much sooner. The new generations of capital ships were becoming ever more expensive and obliged Tirpitz to introduce an extraordinary Navy bill in 1908 in order to alleviate the growing financial plight of the Imperial Navy. For complex domestic reasons which have been discussed in detail elsewhere,[44] this bill had to be constructed in such a way that the traditional building tempo of three capital ships per annum was stepped up to four from 1908-11 before it dropped again to two capital ships per annum between 1912 and 1917. From 1918 onwards the original tempo of three capital ships per annum which had begun in 1898 would be resumed, thanks to the twenty-year replacement clause.

There can be little doubt that the 1908 solution contradicted Tirpitz's systematic plan for naval expansion and contained domestic and diplomatic dangers which he clearly recognised.[45] If he nevertheless allowed himself to be pushed into a digression from his original programme, it was not only because the influence of the Navy League and other organisations which supported a *Vierertempo* had become too powerful under the impact of the encirclement hysteria, but also because it actually improved his chances of getting yet another Navy bill through in 1911-12. The 'gap' of 1912-17 offered an opportunity of demanding a further numerical increase. If the Navy Secretary succeeded in adding two ships to his establishment, the fleet would consist of a total of sixty to be replaced every twenty years. The Iron Budget would have been achieved. But, for two reasons, this was now merely his minimum programme. First, economic considerations militated against allowing the annual building tempo to drop by more than one capital ship. The steel and shipbuilding industry had become all too dependent on government orders and a drastic cut by two capital ships per annum would have had dangerous consequences. The Reich Navy Office therefore believed that from 1911 onwards a well funded propaganda campaign could be expected, advocating a building tempo of at least three ships per annum. Second, by building eighteen capital ships between 1912 and 1918 Tirpitz hoped to reach the magic 2:3 ratio which he considered to be the minimum strength *vis-à-vis* Britain to make the Imperial Navy an effective power-political instrument of German imperialism in the twentieth century.

But the 1908 *Novelle* involved at the same time great dangers which, like the above advantages, were similarly connected with the accelerated building tempo of four capital ships per annum. The first threat related to Germany's relations with Great Britain, the other to domestic politics. The first question was, how would London react to the accelerated building tempo which could only be taken to mean an intensification of the German challenge? The most extreme reaction, which was never discarded by the Reich government as completely impossible, was an immediate preventive strike of the Royal Navy against the unfinished Imperial Navy. The powerful influence of the so-called 'Copenhagen Complex' which resulted from this consideration has been analysed by Jonathan Steinberg with reference to the period 1904-5.[46] The important point in this context is that the spectra of a 'Copenhagen' continued to haunt the Reich government and constituted one element in its diplomacy towards Britain in the years after 1908. On the other hand, London had hitherto responded to the German challenge not by destroying the German fleet in war, but by engaging the Reich in a qualitative and quantitative arms race. But this arms race likewise endangered Tirpitz's programme. It pushed the financial spiral upwards and any attempt by Germany to assume the lead in the arms race was bound further to increase competition. It was therefore imperative that Tirpitz did not build faster than the Admiralty, and in February 1907 the Reich Navy Office had justified this need for moderation as follows:

> 'Should Germany introduce a temporary building tempo of four ships per annum over the next few years and for no recognisable reason, the stigma of having caused a fruitless arms race will be impressed on us and the German Empire will encounter even greater animosities than at present when our reputation as a trouble-maker is bad enough. [Moreover] . . . the Liberal Cabinet in Britain will be thrown out of office and be replaced by a Conservative one which, even if one hopes for the best, will, by making huge investments in the Navy, completely obliterate all our chances of catching up with Britain's maritime power within a measurable space of time.'[47]

As has been mentioned above, the Reich Navy Office chose to ignore these perceptive considerations. In 1908 the building tempo was stepped up to four capital ships per annum. Although the Liberals were not 'thrown out of office', the pressure of public opinion to respond to the new German challenge grew so irresistible that the Cabinet decided to table a large Navy budget. Appreciating the difficulties in which this would involve him, Tirpitz now tried to influence the size of the British increases. He knew that the Liberals were not very keen on armaments because the high costs put their domestic reform programme in jeopardy. From the German point of view, the most promising method of reinforcing Liberal inhibitions was therefore to launch a diplomatic 'peace' offensive.

An analysis of the relevant German files shows that embracing the opponent was precisely the strategy which Tirpitz tried to pursue between 1907 and 1911.[48] He was at first supported in this strategy by the Reich Chancellor who may have been a bit slow in recognising the implications of the 'gap' of 1912-17. At any rate, by making friendly noises towards Britain, the Reich government was not only hoping to avoid a 'Copenhagen', but also to convince the Liberal Cabinet that very large naval increases were really unnecessary. Yet it is more than doubtful that the Kaiser and his advisers were guided by a genuine desire for an Anglo-German understanding. The documents rather seem to support the conclusion that they merely wanted to take some of the heat out of the arms race and to prevent a further deterioration of Anglo-German relations. A limitation of naval armaments which was so widely talked about between 1908 and 1910 was certainly never seriously contemplated by Tirpitz. His calculations as well as Bülow's emerge from a letter which the Reich Chancellor sent to the Kaiser in

August 1908.[49] Bülow started by assuring the monarch that he continued to regard the protection of the naval armaments programme against internal and external vicissitudes as one of his main tasks. According to the German Ambassador in London, he went on, Britain did not intend to wage a preventive war against Germany, but was seeking an Anglo-German understanding on naval questions. Although the Reich government could not adopt such ideas as official policy, Bülow thought it unwise to destroy all British hopes of an agreement.[50] If the Germans took a hard line even in private conversations, he concluded, there would be an increased danger of war or — what was no less disastrous — of 'a colossal [British] programme'. Although he did not fear war as such, he was also concerned, he said, that the Kaiser's life work, the expansion of the navy, could be safely completed. For this reason 'getting through the next few years' was of primary importance.

Bülow repeated this objective four months later in a marginal comment on a letter by Tirpitz.[51] Summarising his policy since 1897, the Navy Secretary stated that he had pursued the idea of building a risk fleet against Britain for a full decade now. In so doing, he had always been aware of the fact that Germany's foreign relations would inevitably pass through a 'danger zone'. During this period of naval construction, he continued, crises such as the present one were bound to arise and there was no reason for panic. On the contrary, the programme which had been adopted should now be executed with 'unflinching energy' (*eiserner Energie*). A revision of the Navy Law would not, at this moment, result in an improvement of the difficult political situation, and in a few years' time the German fleet, if completed as planned, would pose a serious military threat to Britain. Bülow concluded from this outline of Tirpitz's political strategy: 'The task is to get through these years.'

This was easier said than done. Tirpitz's strategy worked to the extent that war was in fact avoided. Moreover, he also succeeded in wrecking an Anglo-German naval understanding which threatened his projected bill of 1912. But closer examination will show that these 'successes' were bought at a very high price indeed. To begin with, the Anglo-German naval arms race continued at an even faster pace. After the 1908 Navy Law which had generated a great deal of disquiet in Britain, the Liberal Cabinet made a last all-out attempt to come to an agreement with the Reich. But both Sir Charles Hardinge and David Lloyd George who travelled to Germany in the summer of 1908 returned empty handed.[52] What followed was a naval programme which demonstrated to the Germans the superior industrial power and the impressive wealth of the British Empire, just as Ballin had predicted. Under the impact of the famous Navy Scare of 1909, Parliament approved four capital ships plus four optional ones, all of which were finally laid down. British industry and the Royal Navy showed themselves capable of planning and constructing no less that eight dreadnoughts at a time and, what was equally astonishing, at a pace which the overworked Imperial Design Bureau and German shipyards were merely dreaming of. This feat left the Germans breathless and — in conjunction with British entente policy and the adoption of the Wide Blockade — destroyed Tirpitz's hope of using the completed German battle fleet as a lever against the first sea power.

At home Tirpitz's strategy also ran into difficulties. The British Navy Scare was grist to the mills of those forces in the Reich which considered a continuation of the arms race too dangerous, or too costly, or both and therefore began to advocate a *rapprochement* at the expense of the Imperial Navy. It is even possible that Tirpitz had primarily this growing opposition in mind when he and Bülow launched their 'peace' offensive towards Britain. He realised that, if the domestic opposition to the navy became too strong, it might prove impossible to get another bill through the Reichstag in 1912. One major reason why these anti-Tirpitz feelings were gathering momentum was that the Reich was, by this time, carrying foward a huge deficit.[53] The increasing pressure to balance it raised the thorny issue of taxes, and it has already been discussed in what way this exerted a destabilising influence on the entire political system.[54] Since armaments were largely responsible for the deficit, it is not surprising that the political parties began to think of ways and means of reducing it.

It is fairly certain that Bülow, a close collaborator of Tirpitz since 1897, was among the first to be vexed by doubts. More and more his own political survival came to depend on a successful solution of the financial question. He knew that the 1908 bill had torn a fresh hole in the Reich Budget and had diminished the chances of success of his proposed tax reform. Moreover, he was moved by fears of a military confrontation between Britain and Germany for which, as Tirpitz had told him, the Imperial Navy was totally unprepared.[55] As early as 1907, he had therefore asked the Navy Secretary impatiently:[56] 'When at last will you have progressed with your fleet far enough so that . . . the *intolerable political* situation may be relieved?' It is against the background of such doubts that we must also see the Chancellor's sudden interest in the arguments of a retired vice-admiral, Karl Galster, who propounded the idea of a fleet of torpedo boats and submarines. A navy of this kind was obviously less menacing to Britain and above all less expensive. Finally, and much to the annoyance of Tirpitz, Bülow also began to look for an Anglo-German detente during the last months of his chancellorship.[57]

Such military and political alternatives to the arms race were, of course, also not lost on the Reichstag deputies. The conservatives especially had much to fear from a tax reform which the 1908 *Novelle* had made inevitable and which could be expected to include direct taxation. Until now naval armaments had been financed almost exclusively through indirect taxes. But there was a limit to putting the major burden of the Kaiser's naval and world policy on the shoulders of the lower classes. Most reasonable people had therefore come round to the view that direct taxation, such as a fully fledged death duty,[58] was politically and socially unavoidable. The agrarians, on the other hand, argued that a death duty would ruin them economically. Not surprisingly, their attitude towards the fleet now began to change. The advantageous revision of agricultural tariffs in 1902, which their approval of the 1898 and 1900 Navy Laws had facilitated, was quickly forgotten by the agrarians when the tax problem began to loom on the horizon. In December 1907, Turpitz saw reason to complain about the 'cold hearted' attitude of the Conservatives towards the navy.[59] An article in *Kreuz-Zeitung* of September 1908 led the Navy Secretary to the conclusion 'that important forces are at work to cut back the development of the Fleet'.[60] The article, he continued, was written by an expert, and rather irksome. It used statements made by Bismarck against the navy and maintained that the construction costs of three capital ships would be sufficient to maintain five army corps. Moreover, the article made the Navy Laws responsible for the deterioration in Anglo-German relations.

Similar doubts about the wisdom of the naval arms race were soon voiced in other parties. On 12 December 1908 Tirpitz noted that the Reichstag was developing 'a mania for economy which could be dangerous'.[61] The Navy Law, or at least the current building tempo of four ships per annum, were in his view threatened. But he decided to resist cuts in the navy budget, at any rate where they touched the principles on which the expansion of the fleet had been based since the turn of the century. To make things worse, Tirpitz now also encountered strong criticism from inside the service and this opposition posed another threat to his idea of filling the 'gap' of 1912-17. For many years now the fleet commands had been suffering from the concentration of all resources on a numerical increase of the battle fleet. All other requirements had been mercilessly curtailed in the face of this priority.[62] There existed an acute shortage of personnel and equipment; officers and men were constantly overworked. The Reich Navy Office had time and again silenced the dissatisfaction with this state of affairs by promising that the eventual completion of the building programme would bring relief. Yet, the beginning of the *qualitative* arms race had obliterated this expectation, like so many others, and the completion of the programme was still not in sight. Above all, the Imperial Navy was quite unprepared for what it was actually being built for: the confrontation with Britain. This feeling of inferiority was psychologically intolerable, especially at a time when many people expected a serious Anglo-German crisis at any moment.[63] In short, the nerves of the naval officer corps were getting very taut. There was less and less sympathy for Tirpitz who dumped one new dreadnought after another on the fleet commands without, at the same time, providing the required manpower and material support. Was it not better to use the scarce resources for improving military preparedness instead of pumping them into the construction of bigger and bigger ships?

This question was the basic motivation behind two memoranda by the fleet commands which the Kaiser received at the end of 1908. They showed that there existed serious doubts within the service not only 'about the wisdom of the policy which the Navy Secretary has adopted for the development of the fleet [but also] about the general defence capabilities of the Reich against naval attack'.[64] Tirpitz was rather dismayed by this criticism. But it merely confirmed him in his view that ' "to hold out" was still the best' until the 'gap' of 1912-17 arose.[65] 'To abandon the ultimate aim and to drop the Navy Law' was now, Tirpitz thought, 'just as unacceptable as using my name for covering up a humiliation.'[66] Unwilling to resign, the Navy Secretary decided to fight his opponents inside and outside the government. He refused to leave his post until the 'storm against the foundations [of the navy]' had subsided.[67] 'The reaction against the huge expenditure', he added, 'has only just set in and is receiving strong support by the threatening posture of England.'

In view of these problems, it was vital from Tirpitz's standpoint that Britain should be kept hopefully waiting and that the 1909 tax reform should create enough additional revenue to cover not only the existing deficit, but also the projected 1912 Navy bill. The agrarians, on the other hand, were prepared to deal the naval armaments programme another blow rather than accept a fully fledged death duty. They objected to the view that direct taxation was the only reasonable way out of the financial mess, preferring short term advantages to a more equitable distribution of tax burdens, even if this meant increasing social tensions. Their rejection of Bülow's financial reforms in 1909 shook the alliance which had existed since 1907 between the right and the liberal parties. The revised tax programme which the agrarians subsequently ratified with the help of the Centre party ruined the relations with the National Liberals and the Left Liberals for good. The collapse of the Bülow bloc ended the Chancellor's political career.[68] But it was also a defeat for Tirpitz, in so far as the revised tax bill barely covered the existing deficit. The implications of this for the projected Navy bill of 1912 were put as follows in a letter which the State Secretary of the Reich Treasury circulated on 26 August 1909.[69] His colleagues would have to understand, Wermuth argued, 'that the internal fibre of the Reich, its defence capabilities and its external prestige require not merely a standstill, but a vigorous reduction of expenditure'. Otherwise the present development would lead 'inexorably to a total collapse of the financial system and of all national activities dependent on it'. Or to put it more bluntly: either Germany de-escalated her ambitious naval and world policy which swallowed a major portion of the Reich Budget or else she would be faced with domestic paralysis. This was the extent of the disintegration which Tirpitz's grand design had meanwhile inflicted on the Prusso-German political system as a whole.

When Theobald von Bethmann Hollweg was made Chancellor in the summer of 1909, one of his main tasks was to put a brake on the process of disintegration and polarisation in domestic policies.[70] This appeared all the more necessary since Reichstag elections were due to be held in two years' time. If he did not succeed in reconciling the parties of the Centre and of the Right and in reversing the widespread disillusionment with the government, a further weakening of the conservatives, the indispensable pillar of the monarchy, and a strengthening of those opposition parties which advocated social and political reform was to be expected. And as Bethmann could not possibly exclude the agrarians and base himself on left-wing majorities in the Reichstag, an electoral victory of the Left threatened to immobilise the entire political system. A *Staatsstreich* was no realistic alternative because of the internal and external risks involved.

In view of these complications there was but one path open to the Chancellor and that was to avoid stirring up the financial question. It had been the awkward tax problem which had caused the fiasco of 1909. It was also prudent to manoeuvre cautiously in the diplomatic field after the connection between the desolate state of Reich finance and the Anglo-German naval arms race had become obvious to everyone. The logical conclusion from this was to put out feelers towards Britain soon after the new chancellor had come to power. In the summer and autumn of 1909 various proposals were drawn up for a *rapprochement* between Britain and Germany. But the British reaction as well as the contributions which Tirpitz made to the internal discussions appear to have convinced Bethmann fairly quickly that this was not a propitious time for negotiations.[71] For the Liberal Cabinet the question of a limitation of naval armaments took precedence over all other topics of possible mutual interest. But from the British point of view 1912 was the crucial year when the German building tempo was due to drop to two capital ships per annum. If the Germans could be nailed down to this tempo, a genuine reduction of armaments could be achieved and, what was even more valuable, the calculations on which Tirpitz's programme was based would be effectively obliterated.

Tirpitz, on the other hand, knew that he had to fill the 'gap' of 1912-17, if he was ever to reach the vital 2:3 ratio or, at least, the *Marineaeternat*.72 He had to try everything to sabotage an Anglo-German understanding at his expense and to get another bill through the Reichstag. If he failed, his life work would lie in ruins. In these circumstances, the year 1912 was of great significance, though for opposite reasons, for both the advocates of a limitation of armaments and the protagonists of a further expansion of the Imperial Navy.

In the winter of 1910-11 the Reich Navy Office, quite consistently with the policy, began to prepare the 1912 bill. Personnel increases which were supposed to please the fleet commands apart, the plan envisaged the addition of six capital ships, bringing the building tempo for 1912-17 up from two to three per annum. These preparations received a fresh boost after the second Moroccan crisis which, the Reich Navy Office believed, would, whatever its outcome, have a favourable effect on the public reception of the projected Navy bill. On the other hand, it was clear that the announcement of the bill would immediately raise the tax issue which had caused so much bad blood in 1909. Reichstag elections were due to be held in January 1912 and Bethmann Hollweg was reluctant to publish unpopular tax increases before then. The Conservatives were as strictly opposed to direct taxation as ever and both the Reich Chancellor and the Secretary of the Treasury were most unhappy about Tirpitz's plans. They feared a landslide victory of the Left and were under no illusion about the effect which this would have on the stability of the monarchy. Bethmann therefore had to try to prevent the publication of the Navy bill prior to the elections and to whittle down its size in the meantime. Such a reduction seemed possible. Tirpitz's six additional ships were the optimum, and Bethmann had discovered that, even if four ships were struck off, the navy would still obtain its minimum establishment of sixty, the famous *Marineaeternat*.

We cannot here discuss the interdepartmental struggle which took place in the winter of 1911-12 between the Reich Chancellery and the Reich Treasury on the one hand and the navy on the other.73 The outcome was that Tirpitz was forced to abandon one projected capital ship after another, and by the time of Haldane's visit to Berlin,74 the navy's programme had been cut back to three additional ships. Tirpitz felt he could not make any further concessions. He opposed reductions both in personnel increases and in capital ships and decided to wreck the Haldane Mission which he knew to have a chance of success only if his bill was dropped altogether. As is well known, he succeeded in this objective as well as in getting his truncated bill through the Reichstag. Walther Hubatsch considers this outcome to represent the 'culmination of German naval policy' before 1914.75 But this is taking rather too narrow an approach to the problem of Tirpitz's armaments programme. If one surveys the political battlefield on which the Navy Secretary won his victory, the Kaiser found himself amid ruins: the finances of the Reich were in a most pitiful state; the parties which had once formed the basis of the *Sammlung* were hopelessly divided; the SPD whose programme directly challenged the existing order had become the largest party in the Reichstag; the confidence in Tirpitz's prognoses had disappeared; the navy had ceased to be the admired object of the nation; the prestige of the Crown and of William II which the naval programme had been designed to augment had suffered a severe setback; the influence of the Reichstag had not been reduced as planned; the Reich's relations with Britain were badly damaged and an end to 'encirclement' was not in sight. Above all, it had become evident that Germany lacked the stamina to achieve her ambitious aims. The British, it is true, were also groaning under the burden of armaments.[76] But there was never any doubt that they would make every sacrifice to preserve their hegemony at sea and the balance of power on the European continent. In Germany, on the other hand, few people were in a sacrificial mood, least of all the agrarians. On the contrary, the tax question had kindled latent social conflicts. In short, German naval policy had lost its erstwhile domestic and foreign policy function. Worse still, it had directly contributed to the sorry state of the monarchy at home and the desperate predicament abroad.

The history of naval armaments after 1912 shows that the Kaiser and his advisers were gradually becoming aware of this negative balance sheet. There were two factors, Tirpitz wrote in April 1914, 'which have caused the unfortunate setbacks of recent years'.[77] First of all there was the 1908 *Novelle* and the 'gap' of 1912-17 which could not be adequately filled in 1912. Second, there was the 'exploitation of the gap by the extraordinarily active British Navy Minister Churchill who — this his enemy is bound to admit — has raised the standard of the Royal Navy to an unusually high level'. Tirpitz made several desperate attempts to counteract Churchill's activities. Thus he prepared another bill in the winter of 1912-13 which was intended 'to re-establish the [original] building tempo of three capital ships' per annum.[78] It is indicative of the extent to which Tirpitz's grand design had collapsed that the opposition of the Reich Chancellery and other authorities to this plan met with immediate success. The programme was shelved without much ado.

One contributing factor in this was that the critics inside the navy had not been silenced by the personnel increases of 1912. 'Under the pressure of the [1912] Army bill and of the financial situation', the Reich Navy Office had been forced to restrict its claims 'to the absolute minimum'.[79] Consequently the fleet commands were no better off than before. As one officer who was sent out to examine the problems of the 'front line' reported, people were 'at present completely exhausted by the work of the current fiscal year; everything has been mobilised to the last man to man the ships. Hardly any personnel is left on land.' And everywhere, Oldekop concluded his report, he had heard loud complaints about the appalling service conditions.[80]

To this depressing state of affairs must be added the fact that Britain continued the qualitative arms race. At the end of November 1912 reports were reaching Berlin that the Admiralty was thinking of equipping the Royal Navy with 15-inch guns and over.[81] There was no scope for such increases in the navy budget. When, in the following year, the German Naval Attache tried to reassure the Kaiser that the trend towards bigger calibres might soon be reversed, William jotted in the margin of the report:[82] 'That would be a blessing.' His brother, Prince Henry of Prussia, had long come to the conclusion that the construction costs of dreadnoughts had become prohibitive.[83] As the Chief of the Naval Cabinet added, Prince Henry had 'tacitly given up hope a good while ago that the aims of Your Majesty's naval policy can be achieved through [building] dreadnoughts'.[84] By November 1913 even the Kaiser was getting frightened by 'this spiral without end'.[85] In short, he had at last come to appreciate the ruinous character of the Anglo-German naval arms race.

Faced with mounting difficulties, Tirpitz now tried to rescue as much as possible from the wreckage of his original programme and clung, in theory at least, to the 16:10 ratio which the Admiralty had proclaimed to be a sufficient margin of safety for the Royal Navy. In practice, Britain retained her superiority at sea and, by adopting the Wide Blockade, also flouted the strategic calculations on which the Tirpitz Plan was based. It did not take the experience of the First World War for the Reich government to recognise the depressing German naval position *vis-à-vis* Britain, although some people's illusions proved rather persistent. As late as March 1912, William II was showing little appreciation of British economic resources, as is evidenced by his reaction to a report from London on Britain's alleged difficulties in continuing the arms race. 'We have them at the wall', the Kaiser rejoiced.[86] A few months later, he offered another revealing comment on the ultimate aims of German naval policy when being told of Grey's intention 'to maintain approximately the balance of power' in Europe. '[That] will change', he wrote.[87]

Yet a change in Germany's favour never took place and by 1913 the opponents of the Navy Secretary found it less and less difficult to convince the monarch of the perniciousness of the fleet programme. At first the projected bill of 1913 was postponed. Then, in August 1913, Tirpitz was asked by the Treasury to reduce, where possible, naval expenditure for 1914, and 'under no circumstances' should the Reich Navy Office exceed the approved estimates.[88] Of course, the Navy Secretary protested, arguing that more personnel were needed to cope with the advanced technology of dreadnoughts. But such arguments had little effect. Too many people in the government had come to realise that the navy had failed to pay the expected dividends. In April 1914 Tirpitz made another attempt to improve the financial position. He told the Kaiser that over the next eight years the fleet required additional funds to the tune of 150-200 million marks in order to be brought up to maximum efficiency.[89] Yet, even his reminder of 'the great historical merits' which the monarch had 'won with regard to the creation of the fleet' did not get him anywhere.[90] After Bethmann's attitude towards the Navy Secretary had long become one of 'open hostility', the Kaiser and the Army, 'especially the Chief of the General Staff v. Moltke', also no longer trusted him.[91]

Increasingly isolated, Tirpitz repeatedly thought of submitting his resignation. What made his predicament particularly intolerable was that he was convinced the Reich found itself 'on a downward slide' (*auf gleitender Bahn*).[92] How could this dangerous development be stopped? This was also what other advisers of the Kaiser were strenuously asking themselves. The idea of limiting armaments and of using a large portion of Reich revenue for social reforms, as propounded by the Liberals in Britain, preconditioned the acceptance of social change. But this was precisely what the ruling elites of Germany were not prepared to accept.[93] Ever since Bismarck, their method of stabilising the monarchy had been to arrest 'the process of fundamental change, which had been set in motion by the Industrial Revolution, with the help of manipulative nationalist strategies of distraction'.[94] Only the Social Democrats, the Left Liberals and certain elements in the National Liberal party advocated a reform of the political system. But they were practically powerless and their activities were impeded by the demogogic propaganda of the Right. And since the monarchy found it so difficult to develop reformist tendencies, armaments could also not be abandoned. For, as Tirpitz knew so well, armaments were most useful for mobilising friend-foe instincts among the population. The socially and politically integrating effect of this had been an important feature of German policy during the relatively tranquil years at the turn of the century. Now, during the last years before 1914, at a time of heightened domestic and diplomatic crisis, integration through armaments became even more indispensable than before. The only change that took place was that the emphasis of Wilhelmine armaments policy shifted from the navy to the army when it became clear that the fleet was incapable of fulfilling its political function.[95]

This reorientation of German armaments policy which occurred after 1912, however, also increased the political weight of those conservative, preindustrial forces in German society which felt most threatened by the growing demand for reform. When the 1912 Reichstag elections resulted in a further deterioration of their domestic position and when the Reich suffered repeated diplomatic defeats, military and court circles became more and more convinced that a foreign war was the only way out of a hopeless situation. A victorious campaign against France and Russia promised not only to achieve a decisive shift in the balance of power in Germany's favour and to facilitate her ascendancy to world power status (which naval armaments had failed to secure), but also to create a unity among the different social classes which the monarchy had failed to generate by peaceful means and without which the political system had little prospect of surviving in its traditional shape and form.96

Before it was therefore 'too late', i.e. before Germany's strategic position *vis-à-vis* the Triple Entente became untenable and before the monarchy slithered into a parliamentary system of government, the ruling elites would rather try to wage a successful European war. If this war was victorious, the external and internal position of Prusso-German constitutionalism would be restored. If, on the other hand, the Reich was defeated, the collapse of the existing order was hardly avoidable. It was due to a 'crisis strategy' which had gone wrong and which is connected with the name of Tirpitz that the Kaiser had to take risks during July 1914 which put his throne in jeopardy.97

This conclusion, well documented as it now seems to be, is, of course, reached with the benefit of hindsight, and it took some fifty years for it to become fairly generally accepted among professional historians. But there was at least one politician and shrewd observer of the German scene who had arrived at it several years before the July crisis of 1914: August Bebel, the SPD leader. As early as September 1910 he was reported to have said this about the situation in Germany:

'To reform Prussia is impossible; it will remain the *Junkerstaat* it is at present, or go to pieces altogether. The Hohenzollerns, too, won't change and cannot change, and when the Kaiser speaks as he did at Königsberg lately, he does so as King of Prussia by the Grace of God and with his Junkers behind him. I cannot understand what the British governments and people are about in letting Germany creep up to them so closely in naval armaments. As a regular member of the Budget Commission I can assert that the German Naval Law of 1900 was directed against England alone . . . I am convinced we are on the eve of the most dreadful war Europe has ever seen. Things cannot go on as at present; the burden of military charges are [*sic*] crushing people and the Kaiser and his Government are fully alive to the fact. Everything works for a great crisis in Germany.'98

Notes

1. This article is a translation, with several modifications, of a paper which first appeared in H. Schottelius and W. Deist (eds), *Marine und Marinepolitik, 1871-1914*, Düsseldorf, 1972. The author would like to thank the Militärgeschichtliches Forschungsamt, Freiburg, for permission to publish it in this volume.
2. For a summary of the debate see F. Forstmeier, 'Der Tirpitzsche Flottenbau im Urteil der Historiker', in H. Schottelius and W. Deist (eds), *op. cit.*, pp. 34ff. The custodian of what one might call the Tirpitz Legacy is Walther Hubatsch. See his most recent criticism of practically every historian who does not agree with his views and his somewhat peculiar use of the sources in *Schiff und Zeit*, I/1973, pp. 30f. Without offering the slightest evidence for his polemical assertions, he is, in effect, trying to put the clock back to the interwar period. He praises in particular H. Hallmann's works of 1927 and 1933. But he does not seem to realise that the latter has meanwhile revealed how he was influenced in his apologetic treatment of German naval policy by *nationale* considerations. Given the political climate of the Weimar Republic and the preoccupation of its historians with the 'war-guilt lie', this admission merely confirmed what people had been suspecting all along.
3. See the articles by P. M. Kennedy and E. Wegener in H. Schottelius and W. Deist (eds), *op. cit.*, pp. 187ff., 236ff.
4. Eckart Kehr, *Schlachtflottenbau und Parteipolitik, 1894-1901*, Berlin, 1930; idem, *Der Primat der Innenpolitik. Gesammelte Aufsätze zur preussisch-deutschen Sozialgeschichte im 19. und 20. Jahrhundert*, with an introduction by H.-U. Wehler, Berlin, 1965.
5. As far as I can see, only W. Hubatsch continues to dismiss Kehr's achievement and considers his own *Die Ära Tirpitz*, Göttingen, 1955, the last word on the subject. See his article in *Schiff und Zeit*, 1/1973, pp. 30f. It will be interesting to see how he can substantiate this claim in the light of the documents which are now available at the Federal Archives.
6. H.-U. Wehler, 'Der Aufstieg des Organisierten Kapitalismus und Interventionsstaats in Deutschland', in H.-A. Winkler (ed), *Organisierter Kapitalismus*, Göttingen, 1973.
7. J. C. G. Röhl, *Deutschland ohne Bismarck*, Tübingen, 1969, p. 246.
8. H.-U. Wehler, *Bismarck und der Imperialismus*, Cologne, 1969, p. 487.
9. For details see H. Rosenberg, *Grosse Depression und Bismarckzeit*, Berlin, 1967.
10. Quoted in P.-Chr. Witt, *Die Finanzpolitik des Deutschen Reiches von 1903 bis 1913*, Lübeck-Hamburg, 1970, p. 60.
11. A. von Waldersee, *Denkwürdigkeiten*, 3 Vols., Stuttgart, 1922-3.
12. J. Steinberg, 'The Tirpitz Plan', in *Historical Journal*, 16 (March 1973), p. 198.
13. A. von Waldersee, *op. cit.*, Vol. 2, p. 309.
14. See on this problem, M. Stürmer, 'Staatsstreichgedanken im Bismarckreich', in *Historische Zeitschrift*, 209 (1969), pp. 566ff.
15. Quoted in J. Röhl, *op. cit.*, p. 199.
16. Generallandesarchiv (GLA) Karlsruhe, 233/34801, Gesandtschaft Berlin, Report of 18.9.1895.
17. This is confirmed by the evidence presented by G. Eley, '*Sammlungspolitik*: social imperialism of the Navy Law of 1898' in *Militärgeschichtliche Mitteilungen*, 1, 1974. His article does not seem to support D. Stegmann's argument about the central position which Miquel's concept occupied in Reich policy in this period.

18. See above, n. 4. See also J. Steinberg, *Yesterday's Deterrent*, London, 1965.
19. This is where G. Eley's criticism of the 'Kehrite' argument (see above, n. 17) fails to convince.
20. In 1902.
21. See V. R. Berghahn, *Die Tirpitz Plan: Genesis und Verfall einer innenpolitischen Krisenstrategie unter Wilhelm II*, Düsseldorf, 1972, pp. 146ff.
22. Quoted *ibid.*, p. 148f.
23. Quoted *ibid.*, p. 150.
24. D. Stegmann, *Die Erben Bismarcks*, Cologne, 1970.
25. On the Prussian constitutional conflict see, for example, G. A. Craig, *The Politics of the Prussian Army, 1640-1945*, New York, 1964, pp. 136ff.
26. For a detailed discussion of the *Aeternat* problem see V. R. Berghahn, *Tirpitz Plan*, pp. 23ff., 90ff., 157ff.
27. See the studies by H. Rosenberg and H.-U. Wehler above, n. 8 and 9.
28. Bundesarchiv-Militärarchiv (BA-MA) Freiburg, RMA, 2044, PG 66074, *Notes by Tirpitz for his Audience with the Kaiser at Rominten on 28.9.1899*, n.d.
29. *Ibid.*, 2036, PG 66040, *Sicherung Deutschlands gegen einen englischen Angriff* (February 1900).
30. *Ibid.*, 2044, PG 66074, *Notes by Tirpitz for his Audience with the Kaiser at Rominten on 28.9.1899*, n.d.
31. Several marginal comments by Tirpitz quoted in V. R. Berghahn, *Tirpitz Plan*, p. 191.
32. See above, n. 3.
33. For a detailed discussion of the *Stufenplan* see V. R. Berghahn, *Tirpitz Plan*, pp. 157ff., 205ff.
34. For details see *ibid.*, pp. 380ff.
35. A. von Tirpitz, *Erinnerungen*, Leipzig, 1919, p. 52.
36. See above, n. 21.
37. It was, of course, always a precarious stability which forced the government time and again to conclude *ad hoc* compromises with the parties over minor issues in the interest of preserving the alliance of basically very heterogeneous groups. The outcome of the 1903 elections in which the SPD made considerable gains was a first warning signal of the greater difficulties ahead. A study of these problems is being prepared by D. M. Bleyberg, Norwich.
38. For details see V. R. Berghahn, *Tirpitz Plan*, p. 305ff.
39. Quoted in *Grosse Politik der Europäischen Kabinette* (GP), Vol. 24, No. 8216, *Bülow to the Kaiser*, 15.7.1908.
40. Adapted from W. Sombart's famous *Händler und Helden*. I am grateful to K. Hildebrand, Bielefeld, for drawing my attention to this. See also Hildebrand's unpublished habilitation thesis, 'Preussen als Faktor der britischen Weltpolitik, 1866-1870', Mannheim, 1971, for an analysis of the causes of this 'misunderstanding'.
41. For a general discussion of this problem see D. Senghaas, *Rüstung und Militarismus*, Frankfurt, 1972, pp. 37ff.
42. A few suggestions have been put forward in V. R. Berghahn, *Rüstung und Machtpolitik*, Düsseldorf, 1973, pp. 70ff.
43. F. Fischer, *Krieg der Illusionen. Die deutsche Politik von 1911 bis 1914*, Düsseldorf, 1969.
44. See V. R. Berghahn, *Tirpitz Plan*, pp. 556ff.
45. *Ibid.*
46. J. Steinberg, 'The Copenhagen complex', in *Journal of Contemporary History*, 3 (1966), pp. 23ff.

47. BA-MA Freiburg, RMA, 2040, PG 66060, *Weiterer Ausbau des Flottengesetzes*, 4.2.1907.
48. See V. R. Berghahn, *Germany and the Approach of War in 1914*, London, 1973, pp. 43ff., 65ff.
49. GP, Vol. 24, No. 8239, *Bülow to the Kaiser*, 26.8.1908.
50. Bülow apparently meant this to be a reminder to the Kaiser after the latter had failed to observe this point during the Kronberg talks with Sir Charles Hardinge. See A. von Tirpitz, *Der Aufbau der deutschen Weltmacht*, Stuttgart, 1924, pp. 69ff.
51. GP, Vol. 24, No. 10238, *Tirpitz to Bülow*, 17.12.1908.
52. *Ibid.*, Nos. 8225ff.
53. On the financial problem see P.-Chr. Witt, 'Reichsfinanzen und Rüstungspolitik 1898-1914', in H. Schottelius and W. Deist (eds), *op. cit.*, pp. 146ff.
54. See above, pp. 72ff.
55. See A. von Tirpitz, *Aufbau*, pp. 97f.
56. Quoted in V. R. Berghahn, *Tirpitz Plan*, p. 585.
57. See GP, Vol. 28, Nos. 10227ff; A. von Tirpitz, *Aufbau*, pp. 93ff.
58. A limited death duty, covering distant relatives, had been introduced in 1906. The idea was to extend this duty to spouses and children.
59. BA-MA Freiburg, MK, 3304, PG 66713, *Tirpitz to Müller*, 5.12.1907.
60. *Ibid.*, RMA, 2045, PG 66081, *File Note by Tirpitz*, 6.9.1908.
61. *Ibid., File Note by Tirpitz*, 12.12.1908.
62. For details see V. R. Berghahn, *Tirpitz Plan*, pp. 331ff.
63. See V. R. Berghahn, 'Zu den Zielen des deutschen Flottenbaus unter Wilhelm II', in *Historische Zeitschrift*, 210 (1970), p. 69.
64. BA-MA Freiburg, RMA, 2045, PG 66081, *Cabinet Order of 9.1.1909*.
65. *Ibid.*, MK, 3443, PG 66473, *Tirpitz to Müller*, 25.4.1909.
66. What apparently he meant by this was an Anglo-German understanding which he thought was tantamount to Germany bowing to British pressure.
67. BA-MA Freiburg, RMA, 2045, PG 66081, *Tirpitz to Holtzendorff*, 20.4.1909.
68. For details see P.-Chr. Witt, *Finanzpolitik*, pp. 273ff.
69. Quoted in P.-Chr. Witt's article in H. Schottelius and W. Deist (eds), *op. cit.*, p. 166n.
70. For details see V. R. Berghahn, *Germany*, pp. 85ff.
71. *Ibid.*, pp. 91ff.
72. For details see *ibid.*, pp. 104ff.
73. See *ibid.*, pp. 108ff.; F. Fischer, *Krieg*, pp. 169ff.
74. For details see J. Steinberg's article in H. Schottelius and W. Deist (eds), *op. cit.*, pp. 263ff.
75. W. Hubatsch, 'Der Kulminationspunkt der deutschen Marinepolitik im Jahre 1912', in *Historische Zeitschrift*, 176 (1953), pp. 291ff.
76. A comparative study on this aspect of the Anglo-German arms race would be very desirable.
77. A. von Tirpitz, *Aufbau*, p. 422.
78. *Ibid.*, p. 365; BA-MA Freiburg, RMA, 2045, PG 66083.
79. BA-MA Freiburg, RMA, 2041, PG 66063, *Memorandum by Capelle*, 22.5.1912.
80. *Ibid.*, 6028, H. 17, *Report by Oldekop*, 23.11.1912.
81. See the reports by the German Naval Attache in *ibid.*, 7188, PG 68943 and PG 68944.
82. *Ibid.*, PG 69125, *Report of 30.10.1913*.
83. *Ibid.*, MK, 3502, PG 67858, *Kaiser to Müller*, 24.8.1912.

84. *Ibid., Müller to the Kaiser*, 28.8.1912.
85. *Ibid.*, 3443, PG 67475, *Kaiser to Tirpitz*, 4.11.1913.
86. *Ibid.*, RMA, PG 69124, *Report of 13.3.1912*.
87. A. von Tirpitz, *Aufbau*, p. 361.
88. BA-MA Freiburg, RMA, 6024, H. 28a, *Treasury to Tirpitz*, 25.8.1913.
89. A. von Tirpitz, *Aufbau*, p. 423.
90. *Ibid.*
91. BA-MA Freiburg, Tirpitz Papers, K 7, *Müller to Philipp*, 27.3.1926.
92. *Ibid.*, Capelle Papers, N 170/1, *Tirpitz to Capelle*, 8.7.1913.
93. See the innumerable examples of this in F. Fischer, *Krieg*; D. Stegmann, *op. cit.*; P.-Chr. Witt, *Finanzpolitik*.
94. H. Böhme, 'Thesen zur Beurteilung der gesellschaftlichen, wirtschaftlichen und politischen Ursachen des deutschen Imperialismus', in W. J. Mommsen (ed), *Der moderne Imperialismus*, Stuttgart, 1971, p. 54.
95. See A. Hillgruber, 'Zwischen Hegemonie und Weltpolitik', in M. Stürmer (ed), *Das kaiserliche Deutschland*, Düsseldorf, 1970, pp. 187ff.; H. Pogge, 'Nationale Verbände zwischen Weltpolitik und Kontinentalpolitik', in H. Schottelius and W. Deist (eds), *op. cit.*, pp. 296ff.; V. R. Berghahn, *Germany*, pp. 125ff.
96. More detailed analysis of this argument is in V. R. Berghahn, *Germany*, pp. 165ff.
97. See now K. H. Jarausch, *The Enigmatic Chancellor*, New Haven, 1973, pp. 148ff.; J. Röhl (ed), *1914: Delusion or Design?*, London, 1973, pp. 21ff.
98. Quoted in R. J. Crampton, 'August Bebel and the British Foreign Office', in *History*, 58 (June 1973), p. 219.

6 THE BRITISH ARMAMENTS INDUSTRY 1890-1914: FALSE LEGEND AND TRUE UTILITY[1]

Clive Trebilcock

Rational analysis of the armaments industry before the First World War has been complicated and frustrated over the last several decades by the persistence of what might be termed the 'Merchants of Death' syndrome. Thanks to this macabre survival, any student attempting to conduct an enquiry from the standpoint of an economic or industrial historian finds himself immediately confronted by a series of lurid non-economic obstacles. Usually erected under titles such as 'The Bloody Traffic' or 'The Pedlars of Death', these obstacles are made up out of a variety of sweeping allegations: that the armaments firms engineered international conflict in order to widen their markets; that they bribed their way into bloated weaponry contracts; that they combined in awesome cartels or 'rings' so as to force weak minded governments into submitting to their sales patter and to their inflated prices.[2] This paper will attempt to remove some of the obstacles and then to indicate, in brief terms, an area in which the armaments industry may have played an economically creative role. To this intention it would be as well to add a cautionary note. The argument which follows in no way attempts to portray the armourers of the *ante bellum* period as heroic figures, merely as businessmen among other businessmen. Nor does it advocate that underdeveloped nations might usefully pursue the objective of economic growth by investing heavily in defence equipment and defence industries. If it is proposed that the armaments industrialists have received over time a somewhat one-sided press, or that the armaments industries have possessed, for several decades, a thoroughly neglected capacity to stimulate technological progress, it is because any confrontation of the industrial record[3] necessarily suggests to the researcher that a trimming of the historical balance is long overdue. The process should clearly begin with a consideration of the charges usually laid at the door of the armaments manufacturer, the archetype of Shaw's 'wicked rich one'.[4]

Arms firms and war

The American Nye Commission investigating the arms trade in the 1930s reflected a widely held and often repeated opinion when it ruled that it was 'against the peace of the world for selfishly interested organizations to be left free to goad and frighten nations into military activity'.[5] But the logic of this charge was not, and never has been, strong. The arms firms could scarcely have 'goaded' unprepared nations, between whom no friction existed, into conflict, and, historically, it has not been private enterprises but governments which have taken the decisions leading to hostilities. Nor could it be seriously suggested that governments have ever required assistance from private enterprise in the generation of disputatious issues. On another count, it has not been adequately recognised that the armourers may not have *wished* to precipitate large scale hostilities. For one thing, their most persistent sales claim – that their wares were effective, above all, as deterrents – would have been proved worthless. For another, they could themselves expect to suffer economically: losses on foreign contracts, problems in international payments, difficulties with raw material supplies, all the dislocations and distortions of a major war, would confront them. And, as munitions suppliers in wartime, special hazards – the certainty of close supervision by the state and the unpleasant likelihood of profit control – might easily have been predicted for them. The armourers' self-interest, much advertised by some critics, might for once be allowed to tell in their favour.

Certainly the historical record offers very little to support the charge of warmongering. For instance, the persistent allegations that British armaments interests worked before 1914 to inflame the situation in the Balkans, turn out, on analysis of the industrial archives, to be almost wholly fanciful. Thus the Letter Books of Vickers Ltd – which in many other ways are very revealing – demonstrate only that the operations of the most important British armaments exporter within the Balkan market were neither large scale nor sinister. Few contracts were received from southeast Europe, and by 1914 only two Balkan states, Serbia and Greece, had featured on Vicker's order books, neither as important clients. Only on one occasion did the British firm become involved in the confrontation in 1911, a Vickers agent, a certain Major Jellicoe, exceeded his instructions and made promises aligning his employers with the Serbs and against the Dual Monarchy. Vickers's reaction was interesting: they dismissed Jellicoe.[6] The lesson of the incident is clear: the armourers did not seek to exacerbate tension; on the contrary, they could not afford involvement in the internal affairs of their customers. Other prospective clients, fearing similar intervention, would no doubt have gone elsewhere, had not the incautious agent been properly chastised. Indeed, there is not a single letter in the armourers' record which suggests that British firms sought to influence the foreign policy of minor nations. Instead, they preferred to find their best customers among the more stable or more powerful governments, those of Spain, Russia, and Japan ranking foremost between 1900 and 1914.

When war came, the British armaments interests exhibited no eager anticipation of impending profits, but were rather surprised and disturbed by the event. At Nobel Dynamite Trust, H. J. Mitchell described the war to an American colleague, in a confidential letter, as 'the unfortunate international complications on this side'.[7] And, some two years earlier, Francis Barker of Vickers had been called upon to reassure an uneasy board that there was little possibility of the Balkan crisis spreading to engulf Russia.[8] For Harry McGowan of Nobel the condition of the British arms trade in 1914 was one of 'the most appalling unpreparedness'.[9] This lack of readiness, the surprise and confusion in armament circles, sits curiously with the charge of warmongering. The armourer who worked for war but was unready when it came is a creation the historian may find difficult to accept.

The attitude of the armourers is not difficult to explain: they did not expect war because they believed in the deterrent capabilities of their products, and they could point to an unusually long period of European peace, apparently maintained by the ever growing guns and battleships, in their support. Only *after* the holocaust of 1914-18 did it become clear that the new armaments could imply an horrific and unacceptable kind of conflict. But for the Edwardian armourers, their trade was much like any other heavy manufacture, and possessed no especially distasteful associations. They could believe that the armaments industry was an essential adjunct to the stability and security of an era. They were proved wrong, but not warmongers.

The arms 'ring'

When the armourers were not causing wars abroad, the syndrome continues, they were exploiting the government at home. The state, as the only customer in the domestic market for military weaponry, was heavily reliant upon a few very specialised arms suppliers, and, consequently, it could easily be exploited by large businesses acting in unison to force up prices. This was the 'ring', a vital component in most assessments of the arms trade.

From the later 1890s, it was indeed the case that free competition was an increasing rarity among the arms firms. A well developed integration process, if not an outright 'ring', was a marked feature of the trade. In 1897, for instance, Vickers absorbed both the artillery works of Maxim-Nordenfeld Ltd and the Barrow Shipyard of the Naval Construction Company, while Armstrongs simultaneously consumed the famous Manchester gunshops of Joseph Whitworth. By 1902 Vickers and Armstrongs were exchanging weapons designs and by 1906 they had arranged a market-sharing agreement covering most of the globe.[10] No less active in the explosives trade, the Nobel's Explosives Co. of Ardeer added considerable cohesion to the cordite industry, absorbing with elaborate stealth as many as five of the smaller manufacturers between 1897 and 1912.[11] A wealth of further examples could be adduced.

There can be no doubt that the armourers favoured any system that reduced competition and emphasised combination. In most accounts this is explained by simple capitalistic greed and the famously conspiratorial nature of the business. The market conditions of the industry have rarely attracted attention. Yet they were very peculiar. Orders, related less to the economic climate than to the wayward graph of international tension, were irregular and undependable. Government officials, ready to invoke the philosophy of *laissez-faire* at the drop of an order book, would do little to alleviate the difficulties of the lean periods between contracts. Entrance to the industry was expensive, the plant so costly that, in most sectors of the trade, only three or four very large firms could afford to participate. And the monolithic nature of home demand erected formidable risk barriers for all producers.[12]

The specialised nature of the domestic market conferred upon the single customer, the monopsonist state, as well as upon the few suppliers, some extraordinary powers. Generous contracts could be used to lure firms into expanding their capacity. Rarified quality standards could be required by way of official specifications. Prices could be manipulated by a client sufficiently influential to play price maker rather than price taker. Faced with this type of customer power, a small number of large businesses will naturally tend to combine. The economic answer to monopsony, logically enough, is oligopoly. Combination may be needed not for the exploitation of the government but for protection against harsh market conditions. The cordite firms of whom the Director of Army Contracts said in 1905, 'If some of the companies are forced to give up the manufacture of cordite . . . there will still be sufficient competition to ensure reasonable prices'[13] could scarcely be blamed for arranging a 'ring' in their own defence. Similarly firms who complained of an official policy which 'manufactured non-employed men'[14] had legitimate reasons for organising countermeasures. Combination offered escape from price cutting and helter skelter pursuit of scarce orders, as well as raising a united voice of protest against highhandedness from Pall Mall or the Horseguards.

In 'civilian' manufacturing at this time, combined action to avoid the ravages of excessive competition and low prices was becoming increasingly common. Such armament 'rings' as existed sprang quite as necessarily from the essential conditions of the trade. Yet where action from the one side was accepted with comparative ease, it was met on the other with almost universal condemnation. The reasoning was less than exact. As the trade press commented pertinently, 'Why the settlement should be *more* immoral when applied to war stores has not yet been made clear'.[15]

Manifestly the armaments 'ring' sprang less from sinister intent than from the peculiar conditions of the market. The critics who have persisted in viewing combination among the armourers as especially vicious have succumbed, as one businessman wrote, to a 'regrettable inability to appreciate that perfectly normal and innocent commercial arrangements can be entered into by armament manufacturers without dishonesty of purpose'.[16]

Bribery

In the foreign market, according to the strident orthodoxy, the armourers did not so much bludgeon with 'rings' as cajole with bribes. At home the heavily defended contracting systems of War Office and Admiralty were proof at least against this charge. Elsewhere, however, the device of public tender was infrequently employed before 1914, and, in countries lacking scrupulous contracting and estimate procedures, bribery of officials, legislators and even ministers could be alleged.

And, in this connection, the allegations were well founded. The Vickers papers reveal that bribery was common when the customers were Japanese, Chinese, South Americans, Spaniards, Russians, Turks or Serbs. According to his telegrams. Vickers's notorious Controller of Overseas Sales, Basil Zaharoff, was 'greasing the wheels' in Russia in 1900, 'doing the needful' in Portugal in 1906, and, 'administering doses of Vickers to Spanish friends', again in 1906.[17] Very large commissions were everyday expenses for the armourers, permitted so that their principal agents could ease contracts through with the necessary largesse.

That bribes were employed by arms firms is beyond question. Of more interest is the significance of the bribery. Traditionally the armourers' sales methods have been judged by the commercial standards of industrialised Western Europe, and, in this context, it has not been difficult to deem them scandalous. The nature of the market — particularly the distant, unfamiliar market — in which these activities took place has again escaped attention. Yet, once more, it is the highly specialised nature of the demand which forms the key to the armourers' behaviour.

One particularly torrid bribery case, breaking in Japan in 1913 as the Fujii Scandal, did indeed reveal that the British firm of Vickers, Sons and Maxim had paid out large sums to eminent Japanese officers and politicians in order to secure the contract for the great battleship,

Kongo. But it also revealed that the giving and taking of bribes was a normal part of contemporary business life in Japan, belonging, as one defence lawyer argued, 'to the tendency of the age'.[18] Armaments firms certainly had no monopoly of the practice: further disclosures indicated that textbook salesmen and electrical engineers were quite on a par with the armourers in their willingness to bribe Japanese customers. The suggestion follows that sales techniques involving bribery may attach more to the market than to the product.

This proposition from Japan is confirmed in a variety of other contexts. The Chinese, as well as the Japanese, preferred 'commission before quality', according to the trade press,[19] and there is a wealth of material to support this contention. One British armaments manufacturer, Douglas Vickers, discovered this for himself on a business trip in 1909. 'That secret commissions are paid', he wrote home, 'is common report and is in accordance with native official practice.'[20] Later he recorded the complaint of a German industrialist that, in order to obtain orders in Canton, 'he was obliged to bribe every official concerned from the Viceroy downwards'.[21] Vickers found that not only armaments but also machinery and building contracts carried the same surcharge. Fortunately, however, the armourers' own testimony is not the only form of evidence available. Corroboration is readily obtainable from the Foreign Office papers. The diplomatic records reveal that concessions as far removed from one another in kind as those for government loans, railways or opium franchises all carried the requirement of lavish 'commissions'. Thus, a departmental minute of 7 January 1896 recorded that the London manager of the Hong Kong and Shanghai Bank did not believe in the credibility of American financial competition in China: 'He thinks the commission to the Yamen is what makes it attractive. *His* Bank do not bribe.' Similarly, a German attempt of 1902 to secure the monopoly for the retail trade in opium earned the comment from Satow that 'this will doubtless include presents to high officials'. The all-pervasive influence of bribery was reflected in the opinion of one Foreign Office correspondent who observed that 'It is a well known fact that up to the present *no* concession has been obtained without large sums spent in bribing the high officials in Pekin', while another informant concluded somewhat despairingly, 'hardly a single foreign firm or individual is able entirely to escape contamination'.[22]

'Questionable' methods of securing orders were thus virtually regulamentary in many markets before 1914, regardless of the product offered. Japan and China are well observed examples, but they are by no means alone. In the Russian Duma in 1913, the country's businessmen were rebuked for relying still on the adage that, 'You will not drive far if you do not lubricate.'[23] And as late as the 1930s an

American armaments manufacturer admitted that 'the real foundation of all South American business is graft . . . something extra is always needed to grease the ways'.[24]

Bribery emerges as no particular adjunct of the arms trade, no sales specialism of the armourers. Nor was it a lure calculated to make governments buy unwanted weapons. It was employed in some areas because it was customary and conventional in all departments of trade. And where it was part of workaday business practice, no mere offer of a commission would encourage officials to place orders that would otherwise have gone unplaced. The process was rather that governments decided to buy arms — or railways or loans — and officials then expected the usual tokens of good will. But precisely because they were usual, the tokens could not of themselves be employed to *create* demand.

Reference to the market context and the basic trading conditions of the arms industry — rather than to the vague connections persistently made between the obviously inhospitable nature of the product and the supposedly infamous methods of selling it — is capable of placing the Edwardian armourers in a new perspective. Powerful objective factors — the nature of international conflicts, the difficulties of dealing with *laissez-faire* governments, the problems posed by a monopsonist customer, the complexities of trade in countries with rudimentary business ethics — were more influential in controlling the armourers' behaviour than any basic drive towards doubtful dealing. Indeed the market conditions of the trade form a central hinge round which this argument, and any accurate assessment of the armourers' activities must swing. For, on the other side, in the area of utility as well as that of legend, it is again the rarified nature of the market which underlies the industry's ability to generate not only myths of remarkable durability but also economic effects of wide significance.

Utility and the 'spin-off' effect: Britain 1890-1914

Market forces acted not only to impress upon the armourers a certain style of commercial behaviour but also to elicit from them a particular form of technological expertise. Under the insistent official demands for new weaponry, the defence industries tended to develop in an unusually research-intensive and innovation-conscious manner. Historically, the pressures to produce advances in weaponry have been stronger than those to produce improvements in commercial products and, until recent times, the research and development expenditures of armament firms have, in consequence, far outrun those of their civilian colleagues. An interesting effect follows: the level of scientific attainment in the armouries is frequently sufficient to produce innovations, mostly in mechanism or materials, useful not only for the armed services but also for the 'civilian' sector of the economy. This transfer of innovation from 'warlike' to 'peaceful' industry has become known in current defence analysis as the 'spin-off' process — although the effect itself can claim a longer pedigree than its nomenclature.

Certainly the monopsonist power of the state in the weaponry market, enabling it to set extremely rigorous specifications for armament products, covering materials, workmanship and design, was already in evidence in the three or four decades before the First World War.[25] Thus the British governments of this era were able to call forth from the arms trade the first modern 'cluster' of weaponry innovations, ranging from the quick-firing artillery of 1878 to the military aircraft of 1909, from the magazine rifle of 1891 to the submarine of 1900 and the dreadnought battleship of 1906. Parallel advances in industrial practice were bound to accompany the developments in weaponry. The highest degree of engineering skill was required to produce a thermodynamic machine as intricate as a quick-firing gun. Equally, the manufacture of magazine rifles necessitated strictly standardised and interchangable systems of repetition production. In order to meet such standards British armaments concerns were required to invest very large sums — commonly about 10 per cent of net annual profits[26] — in scientific research and development. And they did so at a time when British 'civilian' industry was sadly deficient in its scientific capabilities. The complexity of the new weapons, the excellence of the equipment needed to produce them, and the heavy commitment to research would strongly suggest that by the 1880s the British armaments industry had reached a level of technical achievement from which it could profitably influence 'civilian' manufacturing practice. No less than with the modern aerospace industry, and conceivably rather more so, government defence requirements proved capable of stimulating innovations which could be transferred, by a process of 'spin-off', from the military to the civilian sectors of the economy.

Contemporary commentators were well aware of the advantages which peacetime technology could draw from a dynamic armaments industry. One wrote in 1914, 'All war expenditure is not waste even from an industrial standpoint. During the past half-century, many of the finest achievements in metallurgy, mechanism and chemistry have been initiated by the development of battleships, explosives and small arms. The ideal of the ordinary manufacturer is to rise to the heights of perfection attained in the ordnance works.'[27] Speaking of the same period, Lord Weir referred to the 'immense part . . . played by armaments in the general engineering of the time'.[28] This was scarcely an exaggeration. Pressure for better armour plate and gun metals led the armourers to experiment with nickel steel and other specially hard alloys — and enabled them to pass the results as a 'spin-off' to the heavy-duty civilian manufacturers, notably to commercial shipbuilding. New cutting steels were employed by the gunmakers to cut the armour and artillery metals, and in the process these were popularised and proved useful for general purpose, high-speed machine tools. Marine turbines were pioneered on naval craft such as Armstrong's light cruiser 'Amethyst' of 1905 before being transferred to passenger liners. Perhaps most important of all, the riflemakers, required by their trade to become expert in standardised flow production, were able, in their advocacy and demonstration of these manufacturing methods, to compensate for the lack of experience in modern repeat processes which afflicted British industry at the turn of the century. As with the celebrated example of BSA, they found that their expertise in the new industrial practices allowed them to turn with profit to bicycle, motorcycle and automobile production. The chairman of BSA advanced precisely this argument when he observed in 1910 that 'having perfected the repetition system, the company found itself in a pre-eminent position in whatever industry it desired to participate' [sic] — and he concluded the argument by taking over the Daimler Motor Company.[29] In fact many armament firms, and not only the riflemakers, were attracted by their shared skill in precision manufacture to the production of bicycles and motor cars. Vickers themselves had produced specialised engines and gearing systems for submarines, and found that they could apply similar principles to motor cars. This they proceeded to do most profitably by way of their wholly owned subsidiary, the Wolseley Motor Co, in the years before the First World War. By 1914 the armaments industry through its connections with Daimler and Wolseley controlled two of Britain's three most technologically progressive motor car concerns. Consequently, the trade press might perhaps be excused for its ambitious deduction that 'Traction improvements have almost wholly originated from gunshops . . . Cycles and motor cars owe their development to the mechanical perfection which grew out of satisfying war requirements.'[30]

Whatever the truth of such exuberant claims, it should be clear that armament research and armament technology played a leading part in developing the most advanced civilian technologies to be found in Britain between 1890 and 1914. The sustained innovational activity of the riflemakers, powder manufacturers and big gunmakers — which, as the trade press pointed out, 'Government arms orders render possible and make necessary'[31] — converted their workshops into centres of instruction for the rest of British industry.

Spin-off: continental drift

The effect of the lesson was not to be confined to Britain, however. For, in the early 1900s, the British armourers took their place as the world's acknowledged leaders in the export not only of warships and guns, but also of armaments technology and arsenals. A chain of armaments factories strung around the world from Ferrol through Tsantsyn to Montreal, from the Mediterranean through the Black Sea to the Sea of Japan, constitutes adequate proof of this proposition. These enterprises were financed partly or wholly by British capital; they worked entirely under British technological guidance; and they often contained a cadre of British skilled labour and management. Even more significantly, they were frequently located in countries that were economically underdeveloped or, at most, developing. If a high-quality armaments sector could produce a battery of stimulating effects within an advanced manufacturing economy around 1900, the transference of such a sector to a less advanced context might be expected *a fortiori* to produce even more useful results.

Developing countries, as Rosenberg has argued,[32] have encountered historical difficulties in creating modern capital-goods industries and this deficiency has denied to them an important source of technical innovation. But if such capital-goods sectors could be made available, Rosenberg contends, the developing economy would experience, 'an important learning process . . . a technological breaking in . . . an external economy of enormous importance to other sectors of the economy'.[33] Here, the crucial point is that armaments technology in the period 1890-1914 *was* attached to a capital-goods industry which the developing country would have very special reasons for encouraging. And, once a government had chosen to allocate its budget so as to take account of this objective, the wider economic effects would follow very swiftly: as Professor Rosovsky has observed, 'military investment has muliplier and accelerator effects and its impact on heavy industry must be profound'.[34]

Significantly, considerations of this kind were not entirely lost on the governments of the prewar years: some of them realised that 'implanted' arsenals could set up a demand for fuels, metals and supporting technologies capable of dragging into activity a wide range of extractive and manufacturing concerns. For a fee the backward country could acquire from the more advanced nations, along with the weapons manufactory, the infusion of a technology far more advanced than anything in current use within its own frontiers. The gap between the imported and resident technologies could be such that the generation of an enormous potential for 'spin-off' might follow.

Examples of such transfers are not difficult to find. In both Spain and Russia the 'spin-off' process is clearly visible and im each case British armaments interests were involved. From 1908 a group consisting of Vickers, Armstrong Whitworth and John Brown of Clydebank were engaged by the Spanish government to carry out large scale naval work at the dockyards of Ferrol and Cartagena.[35] And in Russia, Vickers were requested to assume the role of technical consultants for two very large manufacturing enterprises — the Nicolaieff Dockyard scheme of 1910 and the Tsaritsyn Arsenal project of 1913.[36] In each case the British advisers were bound by contract to provide patents, designs, technical guarantees and expert supervision, everything indeed that was needed to ensure that the client states received the most modern shipbuilding and metallurgical knowledge. British managers and skilled workmen were despatched to Biscay, the Black Sea and the Lower Volga to supervise the work. On government instruction, orders for such sophisticated items as condensers, marine boilers and high-quality steel needed at Ferrol, or for the cranes, machine-tool motors, locomotives, turbines and generators required at Tsaritsyn, were reserved for the novice manufacturers of the two purchasing countries. And for the still more complex equipment the most modern British, German and American machines were provided to make of these dockyards and factories 'model plants', exemplars for the heavy industrial concerns of Russia and Spain. Most interesting of all was the care taken by the two governments to ensure that the economy, as well as the military, benefited from the possession of the new arsenals. This is most clearly seen in the contract provision by which the Spanish government bound its British advisers, as far as possible 'to encourage the national industries'.[37] That the armourers understood and responded to this requirement is demonstrated by their report of 1910 when they described the Spanish scheme as designed to bring together 'various important branches of the national industry such as naval, metallurgical, machine-building and banking societies which have immediately displayed their readiness of forming a society with a higher idea than mere money making'.[38]

Policies of this type — repeated in Italy, Japan, Canada and Turkey in virtually identical form — could be expected to produce several types of 'spin-off' emanating from British-sponsored arsenals. There is the direct — and often substantial — technological contribution made under the terms of the technical agreements between the armourers and the host governments. The first purpose of these technological acquisitions was to provide sophisticated defence equipment, but their relevance to the general level of metallurgical, machine-tool and heavy ship-building practice is clear. Second, there is the demonstration effect provided by the arsenals themselves, illustrating best practice methods for the equipment and management of heavy industrial concerns. And, finally, there is the pressure exerted on the demand side by the highly specialised requirements of the armourers, acting to raise technological levels within the client nation. For a country in the early stages of its industrial career, the total effect could be very substantial indeed.

The pursuit of British armament expertise, the creation of an adequate defence industry, was for all countries involved a very costly operation. Generally high levels of military expenditure supported and enhanced the possibilities for 'spin-off' to occur. Taking naval programmes alone — for the British armourers were most concerned with naval work — it is plain that important shares of national income passed through the new dockyards and armament factories. Using Kuznets's compilation of national income figures,[39] it is possible to match the cost of the major constructional programmes of 1898-1914[40] against national income figures for *the year of commencement*. Table I is thus able to demonstrate that very impressive elements of national income found their way into such industrial establishments as the Black Sea dockyard, the Tsaritsyn armoury, or the various British arsenal schemes in Japan and Italy. And, in the case of Spain, the *whole* of the 2 per cent of the national income for 1906 passed through the two outstations of the British armament industry at Ferrol and Cartagena.

TABLE 1 Cost of naval programmes as percentage of national income and as percentage of total government expenditure

Country	Programme	Cost current prices (millions)	% NI	% TGE
Russia	1898-1904	157 R	2.4 (1900)	10*
Italy	1901-12	419 L	3.3 (1901)	-
	1913-21	161 L	0.82 (1913)	7.9
Japan	1903-16	300 Y	10.3 (1903)	†
Spain	1906-14	172 P	2.0 (1906)	-

* Regular budget.
† Exceeded TGE, 1903; 50 per cent of TGE, 1913.

Sources: Naval costs calculated from *Brassey's Naval Annual* and Vickers Archive. NI estimates: S. Kuznets, 'Quantitative Aspects of the Economic Growth of Nations, I', *Economic Development and Cultural Change*, 5 (1955-7), 53-94. TGE estimates: variously calculated and extracted from H. Rosovsky, *Capital Formation in Japan*, New York, 1961; W. W. Lockwood, *The Economic Development of Japan*, Princeton, 1954; P. I. Lyaschenko, *A History of the National Economy of Russia to 1917*, New York, 1949; J. B. Clough, *An Economic History of Italy*, New York, 1964; and A. Maddison, *Economic Growth in the West*, London, 1964.

TABLE 2 Total military consumption as percentage of government expenditure in Japan and Russia

			%
Japan	total investment in defence durables	1900 1905 1913	62.7 81.4 * 44.1
Russia	total military expenditure (all types)	1914	35 †

* Central Government Investment
† Regular Budget

Sources: Rosovsky, *op. cit.*, p. 26; Lyashchenko, *op. cit.*, pp. 555, 769.

The allocation of such large slices of national income to the weaponry account naturally required governments to set aside very considerable amounts of their national budgets for defence spending. Table 2 gives some of the relevant magnitudes. Such massive activity in the financing of armies and navies, artillery and dreadnoughts, certainly exerted a marked influence on the economic systems required to provide the funds and upon the manufacturing systems to which the funds came as orders. A context was clearly described by the naval construction programmes and the defence budgets in which 'spin-off' processes, once introduced, could thrive and proliferate.

At this point in the argument, however, considerations of 'opportunity cost' tend to intervene:[41] investment in weaponry is said to entail a cost, or sacrifice, in terms of the alternative 'civilian' opportunities — investment in other goods or services, typically social services — foregone for the benefit of the defence sector. And, since military capital-goods are both immensely costly, and, in the direct sense, unproductive, many observers argue that any 'spin-off' benefits are purchased at an extravagant price. The 'burden on the economy' of such spending is thus reckoned to be high, and it is asserted that the same budget transferred to non-military uses would produce more beneficial results, less wastefully.

Since the utility of the defence industries and their claim to any productive role in the industrial process are directly compromised by this approach, some form of counterargument is clearly necessary. It may perhaps be provided in the shape of a set of qualifications to the historical applicability of the 'opportunity-cost' hypothesis: economic theory may need to be modified under the pressure of certain military and political actualities.

In the first place, a number of deductions must be made from the total cost of the defence equipment before the true 'burden on the economy' can be established. Given the disturbed international conditions of the prewar years, that part of the defence cost that is 'not a burden on the civilian economy but a prerequisite to its existence'[42] will assume special importance — and special size. The *net* opportunity cost of weaponry expenditure will be much smaller than the total cost of the defence budgets.

Second, it is important that the *ante bellum* world did not possess the generally understood schedules of alternatives to military expenditure (e.g. housing, medical research, social security, overseas aid) which make opportunity-cost calculations in the modern context more than merely theoretical speculations. Consequently, as Benoit and Lubell have recognised, defence spending could operate as an especially important 'general stimulus to the economy . . . in countries *ideologically resistant to other types of public expenditure*'.[43] The diplomatic pressures of the period 1890-1914 ensured that there would be a large number of such 'ideologically resistant' societies.

Third, there is the grave doubt, rendered no less acute by the current economy problems of the USA, as to whether sufficient compulsions exist to direct funds into more peaceful uses, once military budgets are reduced. Certainly, for the period before 1914, and for the countries under examination, the likelihood is that the alternative to heavy weaponry expenditure was simply smaller total expenditure. The mechanism for transferring funds from military to civilian use within these states was decidedly weak. To talk of the 'inefficiency' or 'high cost' of 'spin-off' innovations in this period introduces a comparative standard (the prospect of greater efficiency or lower cost achieved by redeploying funds) which these 'ideologically resistant' societies had few means of supporting. And, finally, the argument that 'spin-off' innovations might have been produced less wastefully by independent civilian effort is particularly inappropriate for the developing economies of these years. Frequently, even the advanced nations of the time experienced difficulties in maintaining adequate industrial research capacity outside the arsenals — witness the case of Britain between 1870 and 1914 — and the problem has not diminished with time.[44] Developing countries would have been especially badly placed in this respect and it is difficult to imagine that they could have acquired high-grade technologies by any other means than importation. Since armaments technology was among the most sophisticated of all industrial disciplines, the active interest taken by governments in securing and assimilating it assumes a strategic economic importance.[45] Few industrial concerns within the developing countries had the desire, the facilities, or the trained personnel to provide an alternative birthplace for the innovations that were in fact achieved by 'spin-off', and, furthermore, they lacked the means to attract comparable technological assistance from outside. It is difficult to resist the conclusion that the foreign armaments projects offered a combination of technical advice, demand stimulus, and demonstration effect that would not have been available from any other source.

The optimal technology gap

If the defence industries have demonstrated some historical capacity to surmount the doubts raised by the opportunity cost approach — although this approach naturally gains strength as the 'alternatives' become both more clearly defined and more pressing, and the social and political system less 'resistant' — there remains a final suspicion as to their utility. This qualification has been advanced by recent defence analyses which, coinciding with the final painful stages of the Vietnam War and with the accompanying contraction in American industry, have tended to stress the *small* scale of the benefits accruing to present-day technology from the process of 'spin-off'.[46] Significantly, however, these contentions contrast markedly with the dominant orthodoxies current during the confident and expansionist 1960s.[47] The conflict presents a major problem: which view is the appropriate one for the social scientist with historical interests? Should he redefine his tools of long term analysis as the understanding of these tools changes under the pressure of contemporary events? Fortunately, the dilemma in this case may be revealed as an artificial one. It is the historical reality and not the instrument of interpretation which is subject to variation: the most satisfactory proposal is that 'spin-off' itself may operate in different ways at different times.

The element controlling this variation is the width of the technology gap between the military and the civilian industries: the most effective working of the 'spin-off' process depends upon the gap being neither too wide to prevent effective communication, nor so narrow as to nullify the significance of what is communicated. At the present time, in the early 1970s, it may be that this gap is unfavourable: military research and development has progressed beyond the point at which civilian industry may draw from it useful 'spin-off' innovations — current aerospace technology is simply too rarified to produce effects of any general technological utility.[48] But there may well be points in time at which the gap is more productively located. The era of armaments science between approximately 1880 and 1918 would furnish one example, and, if a modern comparison is required, the era of aircraft engineering between roughly 1945 and 1965 might provide it. There is even a possibility that the 'spin-off' process may have been more effective in the intermediate than in the near past: when the weapons technology is closely related to a *medium order* civilian technology. When, for instance, the armament product possesses technical affinities with such utilitarian items as bicycles and automobiles, the potential for 'spin-off' will be high. In contrast, when the weaponry and the civilian technologies have each achieved a large measure of specialisation, or, conversely, when the weaponry technology is extremely sophisticated and the civilian technology extremely backward, the potential for 'spin-off' will be much reduced. This, of course, would imply that the close inter-relationship of the defence industry with the civilian economy is an historical, but not necessarily a permanent, fact.

Despite the obstacles offered by opportunity costs and technology gaps, it would seem that the armament industries do emerge from this analysis with some claim upon the attention of the historian of industrial growth. Indeed, it is probably true that the opportunity cost and the technology gap have been *less* favourably situated *vis-à-vis* the defence industries in recent times than they were in the years before 1914. The social scientist might perhaps take care, therefore, before he hurls modern ammunition indiscriminately at historical targets.

A modest conclusion might be that the British economy drew a considerable industrial transfusion from its armament sector in the decades before the First World War. Further afield, a significant number of developing or undeveloped economies – some, like those of Japan, Russia and Italy at, or near, the critical take off stage of industrialisation – played host to arsenal or dockyard schemes supervised by British armourers in the period 1890-1914. Like all armaments concerns everywhere, these factories and shipyards were unusually large, often the largest concerns of their type, or the largest of all concerns within the client economy. Through these organisations flowed a technology representing 'best practice' methods to the highest western standards. And, given the remarkable level of defence expenditure maintained by the smaller powers, the flow was constant and rapid. So the conclusion for these cases might also be that the technological contribution of the defence sectors was considerable. Both advanced and advancing nations *at this point in time* appear to have profited from the possession of sophisticated armaments industries. The 'spin-off' concept thus provides a place for the defence industries within the schema of technological development and, in doing so, helps to fulfil the underlying purpose of this paper: to remove these industries from their position as the pariahs of modern economic development and to locate them within an intelligible relationship with the 'civilian' manufacturing sector.

Utility for the British armaments industry in the peacetime years of the pre-Armaggedon phase consisted largely in its remarkable technological fertility. False legend stemmed mainly from the practice of judging the *ante bellum* armourers by the standards of the battered and disillusioned European civilisation which emerged from the war, a practice both anachronistic and unfair though frequently practised. It may be largely corrected, as the industry's technological excellence may be largely explained, by placing the hard faced ogres of the scandal stories in their proper market context.

Notes

1. This essay was commissioned as a synoptic survey of my recent work on the British armaments industry. More comprehensive coverage of the points raised here may be found in: Clive Trebilcock, ' "Spin-off" in British Economic History: armaments and industry, 1760-1914', *Economic History Review*, 2nd series, XXII, 1969; Clive Trebilcock, ' "Spin-off": a rejoinder', *Econ. Hist. Rev.*, 2nd series, XXIV, 1971; Clive Trebilcock, 'British armaments and European industrialization', *Econ. Hist. Rev.*, 2nd series, XXVI, 1973; Clive Trebilcock, 'Legends of the British armaments industry, 1890-1914: a revision', *Journal of Contemporary History*, Vol. 5, 1970.
2. See for example: G. H. Ferris, *The War Traders* (London, 1913); J. T. W. Newbold, *The War Trust Exposed* (London, 1916); F. Brockway, *The Bloody Traffic* (London, 1933); or H. C. Engelbrecht and F. C. Hanighen, *Merchants of Death* (London, 1934).
3. In this connection I am grateful to Vickers Ltd for allowing me to see documents relating to the dealings of Vickers, Sons and Maxim Ltd, Maxim Nordenfeld Guns and Ammunition Co. Ltd, the Palmer Shipbuilding Co. Ltd, William Beardmore and Co. Ltd, and Sir W. G. Armstrong, Whitworth and Co. Ltd, and to Imperial Chemical Industries Ltd for allowing me access to the papers of Nobel's Explosives Co. Ltd and the Nobel-Dynamite Trust Co. Ltd.
4. Bernard Shaw, Preface to *Major Barbara*, 1905.
5. *Special Commission Investigating the Munitions Industry, U. S. Senate, 73rd Congress.*
6. Vickers Archive: Vickers Letter Books, 30 August 1911. This source provides a great deal of material which might be thought compromising to the armament interests. It is doubly interesting, therefore, that it is silent upon issues of 'warmongering'.
7. ICI Archive: American Agreement Guardbook V, p. 153. And cf. W. J. Reader, *Imperial Chemical Industries, A History* (London, 1970), Vol. 1, p. 300.
8. Vickers Archive: Vickers Letter Books, 22 October 1912 and 1 August 1913.
9. Quoted by *Arms and Explosives*, January 1919.
10. Vickers Archive: Armstrong Whitworth File, 'Memorandum on Armstrong and Vickers 1906-13'.
11. ICI Archive: Nobel's Explosive Co. papers. And cf. W. J. Reader, *op. cit.*, Ch. 9.
12. On this point see C. Trebilcock, 'A "special relationship" – government, rearmament and the cordite firms', *Econ. Hist. Rev.*, 2nd series, XIX, 1966.
13. Director of Army Contracts Report, 1906.
14. Evidence of Sir W. G. Armstrong Whitworth and Co. Ltd to *Government Factories and Workshops Committee*, 1907 (Cd 3626), Q 2291.
15. *Arms and Explosives*, June 1914.
16. Written evidence of English Steel Co. to *Royal Commission on the Private Manufacture and Trading in Armaments* (Bankes Commission), 1935-6 (Cmnd 5292).

17. Vickers Archive: Zaharoff File, and, more generally, Vickers Letter Books.
18. *Japanese Chronicle*, 9 July 1914.
19. *Arms and Explosives*, August 1900.
20. Vickers Archive: Report of Douglas Vickers on Trade Conditions in China and Japan, 1908-9.
21. *Ibid.*
22. PRO F.O. 17/1287; PRO F.O. 17/1530; PRO F.O. 17/1398. I am grateful to my colleague Mr D. A. McLean for bringing these references to my notice.
23. Reported in *Novoye Vremya*, 15 April 1913.
24. Vickers Archive: Volume IV of Evidence prepared for the Bankes Commission 1935-6.
25. For a more extensive treatment of this point, see Trebilcock, *Econ. Hist. Rev.*, 1969.
26. Calculated from: Vickers Archive; Maxim Nordenfeld Account Books; The Statist 27 September 1902: Cd 3626, QQ 2210 ff.
27. *Financial Review of Reviews*, March 1914.
28. *Engineering*, Silver Jubilee Issue, 1935.
29. BSA Chairman's Annual Report, 1910.
30. *Arms and Explosives*, March 1914.
31. *Ibid.*, October 1916.
32. N. Rosenberg, 'Capital goods, technology, and economic growth', *Oxford Economic Papers*, N.S.15, 1963.
33. *Ibid.*, pp. 220-4.
34. H. Rosovsky, *Capital Formation in Japan* (New York, 1961), p. 22.
35. Vickers Archive: *La Sociedad de la Construccion Naval* File.
36. Vickers Archive: Nicolaieff File and Microfilms 214, 215, 307. For a more extensive treatment of these foreign ventures see Trebilcock, *Econ. Hist. Rev.*, 1973.
37. Vickers Archive: *La Naval* File.
38. Vickers Archive: First Annual Report of *La Sociedad de la Construccion Naval*.
39. S. Kuznets, 'Quantiative aspects of the economic growth of nations, I', *Economic Development and Cultural Change*, 5 (1955-7), 53-94.
40. Calculated from *Brassey's Naval Annual* and various Vickers Archive statistics.
41. For a more extensive treatment of this subject see Trebilcock, *Econ. Hist. Rev.*, 1971.
42. E. Benoit and H. Lubell, in E. Benoit (ed.), *Disarmament and World Economic Interdependence* (London, 1967), p. 53.
43. *Ibid.*, p. 59. My italics.
44. Benoit has argued that, even in a modern context, a reduction in military research and development would almost certainly bring about a decline in the total quantity of industry-related research and that this decline, even if temporary, could be dangerous. E. Benoit, in E. Benoit and K. Boulding (eds.), *Disarmament and the Economy* (New York, 1963), p. 217.
45. Cf. Rosovsky's view that 'military demand undoubtedly played a larger role in countries which industrialised *after the new technology reached a certain state of maturity*', *op. cit.*, p. 27. My italics.
46. See, for example, S. Lieberson, 'An empirical study of military-industrial linkages', *American Journal of Sociology*, Vol. 76, 1971.
47. See, for example, the opinion delivered by the Committee of Inquiry into the Aircraft Industry (Plowden Committee), Cmnd 2853 (1965), p. 29, that 'no other single industry would have such a pervasive effect on the technological

progress of the nation'. Appendix K also contains an interesting and approving summary of the 'Spin-off' doctrine.

48.   Cf. the opinion of R. R. Nelson in Benoit and Boulding, *op. cit.*, p. 126, that 'military R & D *increasingly* is exploring areas far away from those of clear relevance to the civilian economy'. My italics.

7 ORGANISING AN ECONOMY FOR WAR: THE RUSSIAN SHELL SHORTAGE, 1914-17

Norman Stone

Once military history goes beyond its traditional boundaries, it almost becomes *histoire totale*. Especially in modern Europe, the machinery of state defence involves almost all the vital factors of a nation's existence: technical, economic, social, political, even ideological. On the other hand, it is perhaps worth using the military arm as a test case for the efficacy of government in modern European states. From this viewpoint, armies have many advantages, in so far as their role is a fairly definite one, and can be judged by obvious criteria. It is here proposed to examine the development of government in the latest phase of Tsarist Russia, with reference to the armed forces. In many ways, government was the great problem of *ancien régime* Russia: as Lenin said, revolution would come when the old order could no longer go on in the old way. One obvious factor working against the old order was its inability to win battles, and this may be worth serious investigation.

The Russian performance in the First World War is subject to myth. In the first place, Russians — both Soviet and emigre — tended to agree on one thing: in the words of Professor Mayevski, 'Russia could not, at her then stage of industrial development, meet the demands of modern war'.[1] The Russian army was said to have mobilised slowly, for lack of railways. The invasion of East Prussia was mounted, in the initial phase of the war, to save France from defeat; but it was mounted by armies that were not ready. Later on, once the initial stocks of rifles and shells had been used up, it turned out that the Russian economy was too weak to produce war goods in the right quantity. Throughout 1914, the Russian armies are said to have wrestled with a crippling shell shortage. By the summer of 1915, it had taken on such proportions that the armies could only retreat before *un arrosage d'obus* from the German side: in the summer of 1915, Warsaw, Lemberg, Kovno, Vilna, Brest-Litovsk were given up, Riga held only with difficulty. In the words of Bernard Pares, 'a war of men against metal'. In 1916, thanks allegedly to the efforts of liberal Russia, a war effort was begun, but even so, it could not match the German war effort, the vast quantities of German shell and German guns. This version is well known from the works of Danilov or Golovin, best known among the emigre writers. It tends to emerge from the works of Knox or Pares,[2] or their French counterparts. It is also common in Soviet works, as for instance the introduction to five volumes of documents on various battles of the First World War that appeared in the Soviet Union between the two World Wars. Latterly, it has been given further currency by Solzhenitsyn in *August 1914*. Economic weakness is thought to be a main cause for the relatively undistinguished performance of the Tsarist army in the First World War. It would even be possible to argue, from this, that the weakness of the war effort shows that Russia was not really successfully modernising along the western or semi-western lines suggested most trenchantly by Alexander Gershenkron. Russia's shortage of war goods therefore touches on a central issue, and is worth examining in this light.

In reality, investigation of both the military engagements and the economic performance reveals a surprising refutation of the standard view. What becomes interesting is the adoption of that view, rather than the fact that it was wrong. For two things emerge. First, the Russian army did not lose battles because it was poorly equipped: indeed, in 1916, meagreness of material resources brought it closer to victory than to defeat, because it prompted the generals to think things out — in the case of Brusilov, with remarkable success. Moreover, the economy was not at all incapable of producing war goods: on the contrary, by the late summer of 1916 Russia was producing, monthly, almost as much shell as Germany. Naturally, the consequences to Russia of massive investment in a war effort were probably more difficult to manage than was true of the German case: in particular, there was, by the end of 1916, an almost unmanageable inflation. None the less, the economy, judged merely from its capacity to produce guns, shell, aircraft, gas masks, uniforms, lorries, rifles and so on, unmistakably had developed considerable power. What was interesting was not so much the fact that 'received' opinions on the subject turned out to be misleading, as the way in which the war goods were produced — a peculiar, uneasy, Russian combination of the state and the large producers; it is disorganisation, rather than economic weakness, that turns out to be the central problem.

The figures for production of war goods show that Russia could produce respectable quantities. It was true that production was subject to delay. In the first place, no-one before 1914 had thought that the coming war would last much longer than a few months. Certainly, generals occasionally talked in portentous fashion about the coming Armageddon. This was mainly a way of giving themselves airs. In their own plans, all assumed that the war would be short and that victory must be won at once: indeed, by assuming this they all made blunders that the nature of the war showed to be disastrous. For war production, this calculation was a terrible mistake. Generals wanted shell for six months. Quantities like this were best bought from the existing suppliers – Vickers, Krupp, Schneider, Putilov, the government's arsenals. There was no point in laying in factories to produce shell, let alone machines to make machines to produce shell, for the plant was costly, and generals on a limited budget much preferred to buy the shell from a foreign supplier to making their own machines to produce the shell. For instance, a factory in Voronezh able to give 20,000 fuzes a day would cost 41 million roubles. For the same money, the army could add two million – a third – to its stock of shell. So long as foreign suppliers could respond, there was not much incentive for building large armaments plant inside Russia, the more so as there would be no export industry to make it profitable in peacetime, as was true of the more advanced armaments industries of the West. Russia therefore went to war with three hampering factors: first, a total stock of seven million shells, which sufficed for about six months of war, even then only because transport arrangements were such as to enforce economy; second, a belief that foreign suppliers could be relied upon; third, little capacity at home for new shell – about half a million monthly, at best, when the army needed at least three million to keep going.

It took several months to organise shell production. The War Ministry faced, from October 1914 and even before, huge demands for shell. It reacted, not altogether wrongly, by suspecting that there was enormous wastage; and an expert commission confirmed this. Guns were often being handled by platoon commanders, and would be used for platoon tasks. Batteries would be split up; shell would be kept badly; the High Command had no idea of organising artillery; training was lax. Infantry had been 'spoiled', to the extent of refusing to attack unless guns were there to make an encouraging noise behind them. It was not until the end of the year that any real urgency came into the matter of shell supply; and the shell shortage was written off in St Petersburg as a careerist manoeuvre of General Staff against War Ministry – not without justice. The next step was to rely on foreign producers, in particular Vickers, who were supposed to supply up to a third of Russia's shell in 1915. But Vickers had their hands full of orders. The board behaved badly, took on too much work, was restricted by the British government, and fobbed the Russians off with excuses. As Grand Duke Sergey Mikhailovitch said, 'They have unconscionably lied to us . . . It has been one long, wicked deception.' Only a trickle of shell came from foreign suppliers in 1915 – 1.3 million rounds, mainly in the last three months of the year, against Russian production of eleven million. In rifles, it was the same story: millions of American rifles, promised for late 1915, failed to arrive before March 1917. Indeed, up till then only a tenth of the ordered rifles appeared in Russia. Reliance on foreign suppliers therefore prevented serious exploitation of home resources until the middle of 1915, perhaps in some ways even longer.

Yet events showed that the Russian economy had already, in the First World War, the wherewithal for a first-class war effort. Indeed, what was important was the way war production came about, rather than the simple fact that it did come about. Shell production became part of the political battle inside Russia. It had already been used by the High Command to discredit Sukhomlinov and his satellites in the War Ministry. Once the Duma liberal opposition heard of the shell shortage — details of which were 'leaked' by the High Command — they began to demand the head of Sukhomlinov, and establishment of a patriotic regime able to overcome the crisis. In brief, power should be given to industrialists who understood metals production. An informal alliance developed, late in 1914, between Petersburg industrialists and High Command, with Duma liberals waiting to exploit the government's weakness. In these circumstances, it was tempting to write off the defeats suffered by the army in 1915 to shortage of shell; and from the High Command there issued piteous tales of the state to which the army had been reduced by Sukhomlinov's incompetence: guns were said to have a mere three rounds a day to use against German millions (May 1915); long handled axes were to be issued to the troops because there were no rifles; depot troops could not be trained in rifle practice for lack of rifles. The pressure of defeat made these explanations ever more plausible: the defeat of the X Army in the Masurian Lakes battle in February, of the Carpathian offensive early in April, of Gorlice in May; the loss of Galicia in June, of much of Courland in July, of Warsaw in August, of the rest of Poland in September, produced a mood of patriotic desperation. The Tsar and the more modern of his ministers removed the old bureaucratic servants of autocracy — Sukhomlinov, Maklakov and others — and set up a Special Council for Defence that allowed both the industrialists and the Duma liberals a measure of power. Characteristically, they failed to use it to much effect. The Council for Defence was a forum for wrangling between Moscow industry and Petrograd banks, large industry and small or middling industry, bureaucrats and politicians. Despite much patriotic outcry, most of war production went on more or less as if the Special Council had not existed: the ministries went on ordering direct from the great cartels — Prodameta, for instance — more or less in the old way. Moreover, small and middling industry, as represented in war industries committees, had a much smaller role than their propagandists suggested: together with the semi-official Zemgor organisation, they accounted for less than a tenth of all War Ministry orders, and were generally both late and expensive in delivering even these. In practice, high prices and state subsidies to the large producers stimulated enough in the way of shell production, while Special Councils and War Industries Committees provided little more than political gestures. It was not exactly surprising that servants of the aristocracy should regard them as simple leagues of competing parasites.

Once the decision was made not to rely too heavily on direct foreign purchases, and once the War Ministry appreciated the need for shell in great quantities, the country was able to produce a respectable amount of shell. Russian shell production started later, in mass, than did other countries', but by mid-1916 Russian output was comparable with German — at least, given that two thirds of German shell output had to go to the Western Front. Even in 1915, Russia had more guns and shell, overall, on the Eastern Front than the Central Powers had, though in heavier categories the Central Powers had an advantage. In 1915, Russia produced 11 million shells and imported 1.3 million; in 1916, 23.2 and 9.8 million respectively. By September of 1916, she could produce nearly 4.5 million — a figure not too far from the German monthly total of seven million (late 1916). Austro-Hungarian shell production, which ran at one million per month, hardly counted in calculations of this type, the more so as most of it went to the Italian Front. Shell production was an important indicator of the real strength of an economy — especially in Russia's circumstances, where transport difficulties and the fall of the rouble demanded import-substitution on a considerable scale. To produce powder and explosives was not at all simple; yet by the end of 1916, Russia was producing a great quantity — 4,000 tonnes per month (German: 7,000). By then, there was even a Russian built Haber-Bosch plant working (on the Suma River in Olonets province), which was, even in Germany, the last word in sophistication as regards explosives production. The output of shell was paralleled by output of other war goods: aeroplanes, for instance, where five large factories were producing Russian machines in enough quantity to give the Russian army three quarters of the number of machines used by the French. 'Broadly speaking, it is fair to say that delivery of aircraft was satisfactory.' Similarly, an automobile industry made impressive advances during the war, while the basis of this was an advance in machine tool production that, in Strumilin's view, almost constituted a revolution in Russian industry. It would of course be wrong to suggest that Russian industry could answer all the demands of modern war. Russia was still dependent on foreigners for many of the essential raw materials, and foreigners' production of, for instance, aircraft tended to be superior in quality. Nevertheless, there is sufficient evidence to suggest both that the economy, in its key industrial sectors, was a great deal less backward than used to be supposed, and that the war was not lost for reasons of economic weakness.

Detailed study of the military actions of the First World War in Eastern Europe tends to support this second statement. For instance, there is virtually no truth in the widely held opinion that battles were lost for reasons of weakness in artillery. In the first place, the Russian army suffered from severe misconceptions regarding the effectiveness of artillery in general. It took enormous quantities of shell to perform relatively simple tasks — the Russians themselves calculated that 25,000 rounds of 3-inch light shell were needed to knock down a hundred-metre stretch of nine-strand barbed wire. Even then, the problem was hardly even approached, since, having made a 'breakthrough' of a sort, this had then to be exploited — a task that infantry, moving with painful slowness through machine gun fire, could hardly carry out, and that cavalry, for the same reason, was utterly incapable of carrying out. The great new factor in the First World War was the sudden discovery that battlefield mobility was no more. In the old days, cavalry could perform a useful task — after all, in the Crimean War, the Light Brigade did at least reach the Russian guns. But by 1900, the old type of field gun had been replaced by one capable of discharging ten shells a minute with considerable accuracy up to six miles. Clearly, a horse had little chance of survival, except in freak conditions. At the same time, the internal combustion engine offered no relief: it had been barely adapted to wartime use, and in any case armies had too few cars altogether. In August 1914, the whole of the Russian II Army, victim of Tannenberg, had fifty-two cars and lorries, many of them not in working order. For mass movement, there was in effect only one vehicle capable of extensive use in wartime: the train. Yet this benefited the defender, being pushed back on his railheads, more than the attacker; and virtually every offensive in the First World War came to an end once the defenders retreated to their railheads. Strategically, the attacker was at a great disadvantage, for the defenders' reserves could be moved more speedily to the decisive point than the attackers' reserves. Moreover, even tactically this was true. To conduct an offensive with massive artillery weight was perhaps the only way of conducting one, but at the same time, an agile defender had many ways of avoiding the consequences — dummy trenches, lightly held forward zones, concealed guns, machine gun emplacements. A suitably flexible defence could achieve wonders. As events on both fronts showed, artillery superiority by itself was not nearly enough: on the contrary, an attacker's belief in the power of artillery was the single greatest cause of failures in the offensives, for it prevented, to the middle of 1916 and even beyond, the operational flexibility that success demanded. Staging a ten-day bombardment was simply a way of warning the defenders to move reserves close to the front.

In this context, it is worth indicating that the supposedly crushing superiority of artillery enjoyed by the Germans against Russia in 1915 was not at all comparable to the eventual Allied superiority against

Germany in the west. Although at Verdun, the Germans had had 488 light, 154 medium and 339 heavy guns against the French 24, 57 and 69 respectively — and some of the heavy pieces were old Pange guns taken from the fortress, on the Somme, the British and French had a superiority of four to one in field cannon, two to one in light and medium howitzers, sixty to one in heavy guns. These proportions were infinitely more unfavourable to the Germans than the proportions, even of summer 1915, were to the Russians in Eastern Europe. Even in 1915, the Germans in September were faced by two-fold superiority of artillery; and yet the western offensives of 1915 and 1916 have rightly gone down in legend as costly failures, whereas the German offensive of 1915 against Russia was in many ways an outstanding success. Of course, conditions on the Eastern Front were different, at least to some extent. Russian reserves could be shuttled only slowly — at least in comparison with western feats — because the railways were fewer, and particularly because management of them was, even for Russian circumstances, exceptionally confused. Moreover, armies were smaller, and the area they occupied larger, than in the west, such that the 'breakthrough' could be at least temporarily exploited on the flanks, with large resulting captures of prisoners and *matériel*. But the essential feature resulting from this comparison of east and west can only be that the influence of artillery alone was exaggerated; it was as much an excuse for the generals' failure to think things out as a real factor in the Russian defeats of 1915.

Detailed study of events on the battlefield bears this out. For instance, by far the best known account of Tannenberg — that used even by Solzhenitsyn, as well as by western writers such as Barbara Tuchman — is N. N. Golovin's *Campaign of East Prussia*, translated into many languages. Golovin went to great lengths to prove that the Germans had won because of their strength in artillery; and Soviet writers — the best known of them being probably Vatsetis — followed. Vatsetis, for instance, blandly announces that in the East Prussian campaign the two Russian armies invading East Prussia had 1,040 light, 108 howitzer and 12 heavy guns whereas the German VIII Army had 1,200 of all types. Golovin announces, similarly, that the German field division of infantry was, by virtue of its artillery weight, equivalent to one and a half Russian divisions; by this method, he concludes that the Germans were even superior in divisions to both Russian armies put together. This is all special pleading. In the first place, even if this artillery superiority was not by itself enough to create great successes — in 1916, for instance, the Russian attackers at Lake Narocz had much greater superiority and yet failed to do anything of significance to the Germans. Besides, the Russian writers' figures are simply wrong. They assumed that all German divisions were first-line ones with eighty guns each, whereas a good half of those used in East Prussia were reserve divisions with thirty-six guns (twenty less than even a Russian reserve division), or garrison troops (*Landwehr* or *Landsturm*) with even less. According to the German official history, VIII Army did not, until early September, have more than 800 guns. It had rather more than the Russian I Army, rather less than the Russian II Army. Besides, the Russian superiority would have been greater still had the commanders thought of using their second-line divisions — which they wrote off as cattle — or the reserves of Novogeorgievsk and Kovno, which in the event remained in those fortresses until captured by the Germans in summer 1915.

In the same way, the German breakthrough of Gorlice-Tarnów in May 1915 was written down to crushing German superiority in shell — a view repeated even by modern Soviet writers. It was true that, at the point of breakthrough, the Germans had over 100,000 men and 370 light guns, with 141 heavy guns, to the Russians' 60,000, 144 and 4. It was perhaps also true that each German or Austro-Hungarian gun had over a thousand rounds to use, where each Russian one had forty. In comparison with Verdun, the German superiority was not crushing; and the events, even on the narrow point of breakthrough, cannot altogether be explained by artillery weakness. The Russian troops had failed to create a defence line of any depth: told to dig trenches in a quiet sector, they had merely shifted some snow. The men were mainly second-line, barely trained; more important, the command of both the local army and the army group had supposed that this front would not be attacked. The reserves were all in the wrong place; for, viewed overall, the Central Powers' superiority was negligible. The Russian III Army had 219,000 men to 220,000, and 675 guns to 900. No doubt, at the front of attack the guns were few and poorly supplied with shell; but, a few days before the offensive, the commander of the army's artillery reported that he had 400 rounds per gun in the depots at the front, and still more in parks in the rear. Most of this was, in the course of time, captured by the Germans. Similarly, the German breakthrough towards Warsaw in mid-July 1915 was brought about by German ability to concentrate on the decisive point, rather than by supposed material weakness on the Russian side; here, the decisive failure was in combining the action of separate armies, for the Germans exploited a gap between two armies, neither of which showed much willingness to send reserves to support its neighbour. This resulted in a German capture of Warsaw (4 August); and it was thoroughly unfortunate for the Russians, subsequently, that glaring errors of training and tactics were all sloppily concealed with the excuse of shell shortage. In this action — the Narew breakthrough — there had been 377 Russian guns to 500 German. The German guns had had 400 rounds each; at the front, the Russian ones seemed at times unable to reply; yet in depots not far from the front there were never less than 200 rounds in reserve, and in any case the million shells parked in Novogeorgievsk were never used at all. It is doubtful if even local artillery superiority was of the great significance that military writers sometimes claimed; but in any event, there was no reason, other than clumsy organisation, for even that local superiority to be established.

What was particularly fatal, in this context, was the almost universal belief among Russian generals that, once they had enough shell — according to their standards — all would be well. This was a dangerous rolling of cheeses, for if one offensive failed, more shell would be demanded for the next one. By winter 1915-16, generals thought they were well-off in shell, and Ivanov launched an offensive against the Austro-Hungarians on the Bessarabian border. It failed, with a loss of 100,000 men in a few days. The following March, at Lake Narocz, huge quantities of shell were assembled, and then fired almost 'without system' — were indeed fired blind into a wood, in a thaw that made surface explosion much less effective than usual, while deep penetration of the ground was impossible in view of the fact that it was still frozen a foot or so below the surface. Thereafter, the generals facing the Germans appear to have decided that nothing at all could be done; and two thirds of the Russian army spent the last year and a half of war doing nothing at all — an unmistakably powerful recipe for destroying morale, as 1917 showed. Characteristically, it was on the Southwestern Front, where no-one could dream of artillery superiority, that new tactics were devised. General Brusilov had thought things out. In June 1916 he knew that he possessed at best trivial superiority to the Central Powers; he would have to win by other methods. Surprise, penetration, preparation: all these returned with him to the battlefield. He also recognised that several fronts must be attacked at once, to confuse the enemy reserves, and that the front of attack should be broad, rather than narrow. Maybe the bombardment would be less concentrated; but on a broad front of attack the attackers would not be caught in a pocket of concentric artillery fire, as happened on narrow fronts of attack (for instance, Lake Narocz). There would only be guns to deal with in front, not in flank. There was sufficient in this method to crack an extremely strong Austro-Hungarian defensive line in a matter of hours — just as happened with Ludendorff's breakthrough in March 1918, or for that matter Gouraud's in September 1918. In the conditions of 1916, men wrote of Brusilov's success as having been caused mainly by poor Austro-Hungarian morale. But Brusilov's own invention of tactical devices was a more important factor — one taken over by Ludendorff, without acknowledgement, in the not dissimilar German circumstances of 1918. The success of Brusilov's offensive was a demonstration that artillery and shell weight alone had much less to do with success in the offensive than was generally supposed.

The economy, even in 1914-16, was surprisingly successful in producing war goods, particularly shell. But it was characteristic of Tsarist Russia that the quantities of shell should have been produced in response to a crisis that was, if not imaginary, at least exaggerated. Politicians anxious to discredit the government; industrialists out for profit; field commanders looking for excuses; General Staff men out to do down the bureaucrats of the War Ministry — all had a perfect reason for exaggerating the shell crisis, for forgetting that it reflected rather than caused the generals' bankruptcy of ideas. The shell crisis essentially showed a failure of organisation, not a failure of the economy; and this was shown to be true in 1917, when huge quantities of shell had been accumulated — at least 3,000 rounds per gun in January 1917, far more than the Germans had — and were never used. By October 1917, the old authorities had managed to amass a 'reserve' of 11 million rounds — the whole production of 1915 — of which the Red Army was then made a present. It was on the whole fitting that the Whites, having made the shell in the first place, should then be victims of it.

But if the problem becomes one of organisation, of inventiveness, rather than of economic weakness *à la* Golovin, the historian's task becomes much more complicated. He has in effect to explain why the army authorities were incapable, seemingly, of responding with sense; of matching their strategy, and still more their tactics, to the material position. This would require an almost Namierite examination of the personnel involved; and military history, having lost its empire, has yet to develop a different role for this type far enough to allow such an examination to be made. For the moment, it is only possible to suggest lines of approach, and to take test cases. It is arguable that, in the conditions of the First World War, the relationship of artillery to the rest of the army supplied a valuable test case; for it is clear that, in 1914-17, sufficient integration was not achieved. On the contrary, the 'shell shortage' was a reflection, more than anything else, of confused relations between the fighting troops and the gunners, a matter of fundamental importance in any army.

Before 1914, artillerymen had been notoriously 'apart' from the rest of the army. Their training was highly complicated; they were required to have considerable knowledge of ballistics, trigonometry, materials science. As was the case with the cavalry and the General Staff, there was also a great gulf, socially, between artillery officers and infantry officers. In Tsarist Russia, up to 40 per cent of the infantry officers were of peasant origin — a standard piece of populist autocratic behaviour, common to similar states. Until surprisingly late, a high proportion of the infantry officers had not even successfully completed primary school. For other arms, officers were generally of much higher social position: the General Staff corps, for instance, was recruited overwhelmingly from the bourgeoisie of the large towns, in particular St Petersburg, and the artillery officers were of similar background. Not surprisingly, some disaffection was noted all the time. Artillery officers regarded their infantry colleagues as louts; infantry officers regarded artillery ofiicers as remote, superior, unreliable. In 1904-5, there were frequent cases of artillerymen letting the infantry down; these episodes were of course open to two interpretations, so much so that even to write an official history of Russia's Manchurian defeat became difficult. Artillerymen blamed infantrymen for ignorance of artillery's role and possibilities; infantrymen blamed the artillery for letting them do all the work, merely to save shell. The problem was severe. In the central position — War Ministry or General Staff — artillery officers had roughly their own way; in the provinces, the infantrymen predominated, so much so that the Military Districts — into which the army was divided — did not even have artillery chiefs, merely inspectors entrusted with material matters. Tactics were left to infantrymen, and single batteries were sometimes put under regimental, even company, commanders, with no understanding of artillery's true role. On the other hand, in St Petersburg the central artillery authorities had things largely their own way: they were free to choose what types of gun they wanted, and to dictate manuals for cooperation between infantry and artillery that had not much bearing on reality. The Artillery Department of the War Ministry went its own way, investing heavily in, for instance, fortress guns — many of them to be captured by the Germans in 1915 — while the field army lacked light howitzers, the essential weapon for action against field fortifications. The results in 1914 were twofold: first, a wastage of shell by single batteries, dominated by infantry commanders saving their men some work; second, a belief, on the part of the authorities in St Petersburg, that there was no serious reason for shell shortage other than the unconscionable wastage at the front, produced by the current system. It was this combination, rather than economic weakness, that produced the genuine shell shortage of spring 1915.

In other armies, notably the German, problems of this type were overcome by a General Staff capable of dictating to both infantry and artillery: in Russian circumstances, such a General Staff failed to emerge, at least from the old Tsarist army. The General Staff in Russian circumstances was a transplant from the West, and one that Russian traditions, the size of the country's administrative problems, and the social gulf between the General Staff officers and the others, were likely to reject. The present state of knowledge, both of detail of the Russian army's structure, and perhaps even of methods of historical enquiry that could be used in this context, do not permit extensive explanation of this at the present stage. But it is at least possible to suggest that bureaucratic inertia and confusion, a failure essentially of organisation, and not economic weakness alone, can account for the poverty of Russia's response to war in 1914-17.

Notes

The archival and other sources for the above essay are discussed in the author's recent book *The Eastern Front*, Hodder and Stoughton, 1975. The best statements of the legend regarding shell shortage occur in N. Golovin, *The Russian Army in the World War* (New Haven, 1932), of which there is a two-volume Russian version, *Voyenniye usiliya Rosii* (Paris, 1936). Realities are best seen in A. Manikovski, *Boyevoye snabzheniye russkoy armii v mirovoyu voynu* (Parts 1 and 3, 1921 and 1923, complete edition 1930) and Ye. Barsukov, *Podgotovka Rossii k mirovoy voyne v artilleriskom otnoshenii* (Moscow, 1928); *Russkaya artilleriya v mirovoy voyne* (Moscow, 1938). The battles described are extensively discussed in Russian sources. The Russian equivalent of an official history is the seven-volume *Strategichesky ocherk voyni* (Moscow, 1920-3). The volumes are fairly short, but the series can be compared with the German official history, Reichsarchiv, *Der Weltkrieg* (12 vols., Berlin, 1922-38, and vols. 13 and 14, 1956). A full bibliography of Soviet sources is Lyakhov and Verzhkhovski in *Voyenno-istorichesky Zhurnal*, 1964-72, Moscow. For Mayersky reference see *Ekonomika Rossii v usloviyakh pervoy mirovoy voyni* (1958), p. 63. For Pares reference see B. Pares, *The Fall of the Russian Monarchy* (London, 1939), *passim*.

8 HOW RIGHT IS MIGHT? SOME ASPECTS OF THE INTERNATIONAL DEBATE ABOUT HOW TO FIGHT WARS AND HOW TO WIN THEM, 1870-1918

Geoffrey Best

Later nineteenth-century Europe, in its character as self-conscious pace-setter in world civilisation and on the international side of its political thought, was bound to profess respect for international legality and morality. For non-pacifists this meant the settlement of disputes by non-violent means (arbitration, conciliation, good offices, etc.) when possible; when such means were not possible, by war conducted with all the humanity and civility appropriate to the spirit of the age. Most warmly commended by liberals and (though they had different ends in view) men of the left, this goal of a 'civilised' conduct of war was attractive also to men of the right, including the military, with whose sense of self-interest and ideas of honour, etc. it nicely corresponded. How to attain this goal, and the associated one of substituting non-violent procedures for violent ones, was much debated between the 1860s and the First World War, mainly in print but also on three important occasions at international conferences where military as well as diplomatic, political and international-legal points of view could be heard.[1] This essay has to do with that debate at the points where the old antagonists Might and Right, seconded respectively by Military Necessity and Humanity, reviewed the present state of such eternal questions as: is anything fair in war? what should non-combatants do to be saved? who were noncombatants, anyway? what *was* military necessity? could, and even should, war be made less frightful? and so on.

It was probably in terms of weaponry that any part of this multifaceted debate was most commonly perceived by the political and reading publics at large (as perhaps it still is). The stigmatisation of particular forms of fighting and of particular weapons innovations as improperly 'atrocious' was one of the longest-standing traditions of the laws and customs of war. It had been built into their modern structure by one of the founding charters of the international law of war, the St Petersburg Convention of 1868, which banned a certain sort of 'explosive or inflammable bullets', blood relations of the celebrated dum-dum. Although undeniably important enough to command the continuing attention of sensible commentators and would-be legislators, it lent itself with peculiar facility to the uses of sensational journalism, science fiction, and instant civilian humanitarianism, all of which were then in their flourishing youth. Consequently the growing nastiness of war was apprehended most vividly as a function of the growing terribleness of weapons, and those parts of the great debate which were concerned with the distinction between lawful and unlawful new weapons, from dum-dums and balloon-dropped bombs to asphyxiating gases and submarine mines, seem to have attracted undue attention, both among that pre-1914 public and from subsequent military commentators and historians; 'undue' because developments in weaponry, the means of fighting wars, were no more than peripheral to the real issue: what kind of war was going to be fought?

In retrospect it appears more plainly than it could at the time that the real issue upon which the moral quality of future war would turn was the extent to which 'the people' at large were to recognised as participating in it. The traditions of the major military powers, under whose lights and shadows the international law of war became codified, had strongly tended to distinguish 'the military' proper, who did the fighting, from 'non-combatants' who were to keep out of it. a distinction natural and practical enough, through most of the period from the Treaty of Westphalia to the Declaration of Independence, when wars were formally fought by professional and regular armies and were of such a calculated nature as to be known generically as 'limited' or 'cabinet' wars. The nature of war had, between 1776 and 1870, begun to become unlimited and 'national' enough to press its professional experts to modify their doctrines to take account of it;[2] but on the whole they still stuck to the good old doctrines as offering (so they were pleased to say) less nastiness to non-combatants as well as (this they did not so clearly admit) to themselves, and (this was pointed out only by their critics) as being much more flattering to their professional self-esteem, international aristocratic connections, and vaunted code of honour. Whatever reservations or qualifications might have begun to appear in their theory or practice, their confessed ideal remained that of a conflict between wholly regular forces, applying controlled violence to the end of 'annihilating' the enemy, i.e. reducing his regular forces to the point where no rational prospect of victory remained; not, as our twentieth-century ears unhappily suspect, some dreadful assault upon the civilian population.

Against this theory and would-be practice, an incompatible practice had sporadically been developing since the American War of Independence. 'The people' had become involved; directly and purposefully, as more or less 'irregular' fighters (guerrillas, partisans, the *levée en masse*, etc.), or by the necessary implication of the national war idea, as no less concerned about their nation's fate than their social and political hierarchies. They might even seem more concerned about it, as they were supposed to by the French revolutionaries in 1792-4, and as they more consistently did in Spain between 1808 and 1813, when the burden of national resistance to French imperialism was taken up by the people at large. In Russia in 1812 the people showed themselves at least equally concerned with their governing classes, and collaborated with the 'regular' forces in what amounted to popular and partisan war. In south Germany, Italy, the Tyrol and the Vendée, popular resistance of similar national or regional kinds had shown its power. By the end of the Revolutionary and Napoleonic wars, therefore, there was no lack of examples of the conduct of war in non-regular, non-professional ways, and every nation entered the nineteenth century with a stirring equipment of partly true patriotic stories of popular participation in wars of resistance to, and liberation from, a foreign oppressor.

Yet despite all that, the official theory governing the conduct of war between civilised states, as it developed and tightened up during the early and middle years of the century, stuck as close as it could to the 'regular' rules and precedents, and went as far as it could towards branding the 'irregular' precedents as improper. The reasons are not far to seek. The prestige of the great professional and regular military machines, with all their dynastic and aristocratic connections, was all but irresistible to the diplomats, professors, publicists and international lawyers who shared with the generals the articulation of their civilisation's code of war conduct. Guerrilla war, they insisted (and they were not mistaken!), could hardly avoid being savage. It relied on natural rather than measured violence. It was a kind of military mob rule, that led to anarchy. It knew no laws, was almost impossible to keep within political control, tended to the limitless. So the professional soldiers and the international lawyers attempted, between 1815 and 1870, to brand it a discredited archaism, and to frighten what remained of it into at least a convincing appearance of regularity.[3] Until the late summer of 1870, this attempt had, from a European point of view, every appearance of reasonableness and success.[4]

The Franco-Prussian war reminded the old world of what popular involvement in international war could mean. Neither the French imperial nor the German high commands (nor, perhaps, anyone else in Europe except Marx and Engels) expected to be thus reminded. Napoleon III's commanders were the last Frenchmen to have planned any such thing. When the Germans began to encounter 'irregular' resistance, they were surprised and angry. The war became at once less 'humane' and less enjoyable than they had anticipated. During the months between Sedan and the final armistice, all the usual phenomena of national resistance and guerrilla war appeared: the taking and sometimes execution of hostages to ensure compliance with occupiers' orders; the burning of houses, villages or even townships; the levying of fines on communities, as punishments for alleged illegalities; that ferocious and forbidding tone of public pronouncements which indicated at once the rising of, and the playing upon, mass national passions; the sense, among both invaded and invaders, that they were dealing with an enemy who fought dirty; the deliberate application of hardship and 'terror' (notably, bombardment) to non-combatant civilians;[5] and the rowdy beginning of a prolonged public argument about the conduct of the war, with copious allegations and counter-allegations as to 'who began it' and to what extent it was illegal. This argument was, in common with all such, largely a propaganda exercise. The more neutrals there are to listen, and the more potentially influential they are, the more must it seem worthwhile to play upon their feelings and to gain their sympathy. During this war, neutrals were unusually numerous and, potentially, influential. But that mixture of motives should not blind us to the reality of the moral and legal issues involved. At the politico-philosophical roots of the matter were ultimate questions about human rights and the rights and duties of states to each other in the international community. Perhaps the most significant distillation from those questions into a material point for the agenda of international legal discussion was the endeavour, which persisted from 1870 right up to 1914, to clarify what were the mutual rights and duties of, on the one side, an invader and occupier, and on the other, an invaded and occupied population.

Here was the most conspicuous field on which military might met 'the people', and the one idea of an army (the professional, regular one) met the other (the citizen, national militia one). The question, how the occupying army should conduct itself, divided principally into two parts: the extent to which it might legitimately live off the occupied territory, and the extent to which it might legitimately go on putting down resistance. Whenever the former matter came into debate, the Germans could be relied on to make the largest claims, or, to put it more precisely, to resist most strongly the notion that fixed limits could be set to an invader's and occupier's demands.[6] Whatever may be the other possible or contributory explanations of that fact, it may well partly be understood as a natural historical outcome of Prussia's modern experience (with the most galling exception of 1807-12!) of invading and occupying much more often than of being invaded and occupied, and of a general German determination that this should continue to be the case. It had become part of the Prussian, and therefore after 1871 of the German soldier's confident expectations, that he would be campaigning mostly in enemy territory, and part of the standard German idea about war, that Germans only had to fight when attacked by less peace loving neighbours. Similarly it had become part of the German idea about their soldiers that, having to carry an essentially defensive war into an aggressor enemy's territory, they merited every comfort when they got there. That, at any rate, is my summary interpretation of the causes of the German insistence, whenever the matter was brought up in international debate between 1871 and 1914, that they were entitled to requisition from the people in whose territory they were operating all the basic victuals they needed (and their definition of what was basic was generous, as the Danes could testify from the 1848 and 1864 experiences, and Frenchmen from those of six years later).[7]

But more momentous by far was the discussion about the security of invaders and occupiers amidst their subject populations. Lives were not directly at stake in respect of requisitions. They were when it came to 'resistance' and the conduct an invader should observe towards it. German officials and publicists were again conspicuous in justifying strictness. Their case, buttressed lavishly with Franco-Prussian examples, was that if an invaded and occupied population wished to enjoy the security of life, principle and property to which (they freely conceded) it was morally and legally entitled, it must be absolutely docile and obedient. Otherwise it would not be playing fair! The occupier could himself only play fair by the occupied — dare to spare them from the severities to which his military preoccupations must otherwise justly subject them — if they played fair by him, remaining passively acquiescent to his every order, which, so the argument ran, need then never overstep the lines prescribed by international law. Thus would non-combatant civilians be secured from the horrors of war. No homes need be burnt, no hostages executed, no giant fines exacted, no formal humiliations inflicted; no women desolated; no children terrified; just the legal round of requisitions, contributions and billeting, until the conclusion of peace brought, one way or the other, its final solution to the strife. The Germans never regretted or withdrew from the positions they had adopted against the *francs-tireurs* and every other aspect of the French people's war, such as it was, in 1870-1, and the following forty years of this debate show them arguing tirelessly for the principles they had then defined: that only clearly identifiable and open partisans earned 'laws of war' treatment; that all other inhabitants of the occupied territory ought to be conspicuously non-participant, and if pressed by partisans to help them, ought to inform the occupier about it; that all civil officers, police, etc., would do well to stay on duty and help the occupier maintain order as they would their own government; that all householders ought to stay at home; and so on.

Now the Germans were not alone in this approach to the prospects of invasion and occupation. The Russians and the Austro-Hungarians were of like opinions (which is not surprising) and so also (which is perhaps surprising) were some 'third parties' from smaller, non-military states: Belgium's best-known international lawyer of the seventies, Rolin-Jaequemyns, for example, and the generally benevolent Bluntschli who, though a professor at Heidelberg, was of Swiss nationality. But it seems to have been only in Germany that one significant element of this strong doctrine of occupier's rights was carried to an extreme. I refer to the principle of *Kriegsverrat*, 'war treason', which equated disruption of the occupier's war effort with disruption of one's own and made it equally punishable. This appears to be the highest pitch to which the occupier's case was ever taken.[8] The first modern trace of it known to me is in Lieber's code of Instructions for the US Army in 1863 where it is the meat of articles 90, 91 and 92. Presumably he got it, or at any rate some strong suggestion of it, from earlier texts, and from general principles of Roman Law. Whatever its earlier history, it was brandished a good deal at the French in 1870-1, appearing in many (though certainly not in all) minatory proclamations of the duties of the occupied citizenry; it remained common in German international law books and military law books at least until the early twentieth century; and it was still going strong enough during the German occupation of Belgium for the United States Ambassador to express puzzled amazement at it.[9]

It can easily be understood that this sort of doctrine, despite the elements of benevolence and humanitarianism in its derivation, was odious and unacceptable to the lesser powers, whose only means of defence lay in the general rallying of their population by means ranging from a regularly prepared militia or 'national guard' style civic force through a perhaps anticipated *levée en masse* to a scarcely preparable people's partisan and guerrilla war. There was much resentment among the smaller powers against the pressure put upon them by their larger neighbours towards their adoption of similarly 'regular' armies fed by conscription. They naturally did not want to have to prepare so expensively and deliberately for war. For purposes of national defence upon their own territory (the only sort of war they were interested in), cheaper, less formal citizen forces ought, they believed, to suffice. Under pressure from the international lawyers and the main streams of international military opinion, they accepted that their fighting men ought to wear conventionally recognisable uniforms or, at least, badges, that they should operate under duly constituted authority, that they should themselves observe all the laws and customs of war. What they found it impossible to stomach was that any means of their national resistance should be branded in advance as dirty fighting and theatened with punishment as such. Hear, for example, the principal Belgian representative at the 1874 Brussels conference, stoutly combating the main stream of German and Russian doctrine, to which the writings of his fellow-countryman Rolin-Jaequemyns lent unwelcome support. Baron Lambermont repudiated his view that intemperate patriotism in resistance led to 'banditry':

> 'The Belgian delegate has no intention to become an advocate of banditry and he absolutely repudiates all means of fighting that are not proper ... Certainly, it is good work, to seek to soften the impact of war ... and to conduct hostilities by certain rules ... but you must take note of the tendency and implications of those systems of rules. When every state has got its forces all ready for regular war, when men everywhere are ready to march at the cannons' first roar, numbers will never be on the side of the secondary states. It is therefore for them especially that the mighty power called patriotism matters; patriotism, which makes heroes and which has filled the pages of which all of us are proudest in our various histories ...
>
> 'Defence of one's country [*patrie*] is not only a people's right, it is a people's duty. Horrible things happen in war, will always happen in war, which just have to be put up with. But you are talking here of elevating them to positive legal status! If citizens must be led to slaughter for having dared to try to defend their country at risk of their lives, at least spare them the sight, at the foot of the scaffold, of a Treaty signed by their own government, condemning them to death. These are matters it is better not to legislate about, if we cannot agree as to extent to which persons in occupied territory may legitimately take up arms.'[10]

There was as frank a challenge to the pretensions of military Might as you could hope to find: the counterassertion that a people would be Right in a moral sense, and ought therefore to be regarded as right in the international legal sense, to fight and resist the invader for all it was worth; to hold aloof from the occupier if it was beaten; and *not* to be maltreated for adopting a frankly uncooperative attitude. This sense of Right, founded on doctrines of political rights to national self-determination and democracy, assumed that peoples should be consenting to their governments and forms of government, and refused to see anything respectable, even tolerable, in acquiescence in *force majeure*. It further assumed that no state should wish to impose *force majeure* on a completely defensive and untroublesome people, and that any state which nevertheless set out to impose its will on such another could not credibly deny it the right to self-defence *à l'outrance*. That such a style of war was likely to be rather horrible, its more sensible spokesmen could hardly deny. The rhetoric of popular nationalism, however, supported them with its passionate preference for death rather than subjugation, and reason supported them too, with its calculation that, against a really all-out people's resistance, no regular invasion could actually prevail.

To these arguments (implying a distinctive political philosophy) the spokesmen of the greater military powers (themselves resting on a distinctly different political philosophy) in effect replied that, though none could be more anxious than they to conduct war in legal and honourable ways, their armies ('nations in arms' also, after their conscript fashion) could not allow themselves to be deterred from pursuing their proper war objects by slowing down their tempo, by adjusting their style of operations to suit the preferences of others who might choose to do things differently. If non-combatants were the more hurt because of this difference of military styles, it would not be their fault! So they pressed for clear undertakings on all sides to observe the international laws and customs of war as they understood them and were seeking to codify them, and thus to achieve (as they maintained could only thus be achieved) the distinction and separation of non-combatants from combatants, and the former's due protection, while the regular armies fought it all out between themselves and finished the war with all desirable decisiveness and speed.

So far, it may appear from the humanitarian point of view, so good. Setting aside fundamental political and moral principles, the 'German' military men's argument offered the non-combatant the better deal. But, we may ask, was there not some disingenuousness in that argument? Indeed there was; though it does not seem (so far as my study of the subject goes to date) that it was as much noticed before the First World War as it became thereafter.

In the first place, there was the business of requisitions, contributions, etc., to which brief reference has already been made. The major military powers, the prospective occupiers, would not absolutely limit the extent of their prospective demands.[11] What it amounted to was that the Germans and the others for whom they spoke could offer no brighter prospect to the occupied population than a speedy end to hostilities.[12] In the second place, and more menacing, there was a radical cutting at the roots of the non-combatant/combatant distinction, in the development — the recently very pronounced development — of the principle of hastening the end of hostilities by making the non-combatants squeal. So long as the official codes of conduct of war clung to the old combatant/non-combatant distinction, this growing practice was difficult to formally incorporate in them; but it was there none the less, and as a matter of fact had inconspicuously been so time out of mind. Non-combatants had always been liable to deliberate attack during sieges. Soldiers laying siege to fortified places had always had the opportunity to make the civilians squeal by bombarding them, and had frequently taken it. International lawyers (if that is not too grand a name for the hopeful gropers of the eighteenth and early nineteenth centuries) were never happy about this but produced no clear consensus one way or the other. The Germans had gone in for bombardment a great deal during the war of 1870-1. At Strasbourg, Péronne, Soissons, etc., and above all at Paris, they had diversified their firing on the fortifications of besieged cities with firing into non-military neighbourhoods, and justified it on the ancient ground that the civilians therein were, in those tight psychological circumstances, symbiotically involved with the military and could not realistically be considered apart from them. The civilian will to resist once broken, the military's will would break too.

Nor was it in bombardments alone that this line of argument made sense. In the more advanced modern nation-states of the later nineteenth century, 'the people' at large were inevitably involved in the wars their governments embarked on. The public language of warmaking had, since the French Revolution, more often than not claimed to ground it in the national will. Newspapers, representative politics, and nationalist ideology combined to make much commoner than could ever have been the case before 1789 or 1776 the identification of the people at large with the fortunes of their armies. Wilhelm I proclaimed on entering French territory that he was making war on the French government, not the French people, but soon found out that the French people were making war on him. President Lincoln and his commanders had never been under illusions on this score. It has not been necessary, within the limited European scope of this paper, to notice transatlantic matters, but we may here notice *en passant* that some of the most spectacular (and controversial) episodes of the American Civil War had been ventures into hostile territory systematically, either to render it useless, by devastation, for the enemy's military purposes, or to bring the nasty realities of war home to the enemy's civilian population by ruining their means of livelihood; or, as in the case of Sherman's march through Georgia, to do both at once. The Germans had been driven to put pressure on the French people in a less systematic, *ad hoc* fashion. It is difficult to distinguish the merely vengeful, punitive and angry elements from those of rational calculation in their commanders' minds, but the latter were certainly in the mixture, as the war dragged on beyond the point where it 'ought' to have stopped (i.e. at the annihilation of the imperial armies). Harsh pressure was to be deliberately applied to the French non-combatant population (if it really was non-combatant . . .), so far as it could be got at, in order to bring home to the French in general the fact that they really had been beaten, and that persistence in ignoring the fact would only make things worse for them. From this unpremeditated practice, it was no long distance to the rationalising theory that the distinction between combatants and non-combatants could not be maintained in conditions of modern national 'total' war, and that pressure upon the whole people was, as Goltz put it, its *ultima ratio*.[13]

The final and most conclusive nail in the coffin of the German argument that non-combatants and occupied civilian populations were best protected by 'their' sort of international law was their proviso — a proviso which yearly became more explicit — that the law could be broken whenever 'military necessity' was thought to demand it. None pressed more urgently than the Germans for cast-iron undertakings on behalf of non-combatants, etc., yet, on their own evidence, the Germans would unhesitatingly break their side of the implied bargain if they thought it militarily necessary to do so. To unsympathetic observers, this placing of loop holes at the most vital points of the legal structure looked like a reduction of the marriage of Right and Might to scrap-of-paper status. To German writers, however, it had no such discreditable aura. Other powers, they argued (with an especially meaningful glance at the British Admiralty), did the same when it came to the crunch, but only they, who took military matters with exemplary seriousness and conscientiousness, were ready to admit it.[14] Far from being criticised for ruthlessness, the Germans ought to be admired for honesty.

How 'military necessity' should be defined, and what departures from legal or moral norms it may permit, are questions that have always clung and still cling close to the heart of the international laws and customs of war. Fron one point of view, it seems to undo them utterly. From another, it is perhaps a regrettable fact of life which has to be put up with and carefully watched. Neither point of view is necessarily less 'realistic' than the other. If it is 'realism' to concede that a commander (or national government) may wish to 'break the law' in order to avoid defeat, it is equally 'realistic' to remind him of the longer term (and perhaps international) consequences of his illegality. Properly considered in its entirety, the 'military necessity' question involves aspects of international relations, political science, social psychology and national folklore. The degree of attention given to it by writers on international law and war conduct is rarely commensurate with the breadth of its moral implications. Leaving the attempt at a more adequate study of it until some later occasion, I cannot here do more than confess to an impression that it came to attract increasingly close attention, and to be given an increasingly hard definition, soon after the end of the Franco-Prussian War. This could well have been by natural process of reaction to the current booms in internationalism (everything from the improved organisation of international law and lawyers to the much more publicised pacifist, peace and interparliamentary movements) and what German military writers picked out for specially cautious handling, 'humanitarianism'. Old Moltke touched on both these dangers, as he saw them, in the public letter he wrote to Bluntschli in 1880; a letter which was endlessly quoted by the military-minded as a sort of inspired writing during the next thirty years.[15] Another authoritative militarist text of that period was the series of three articles in the 1877-8 *Deutsche Rundschau* by General Julius von Hartmann on 'Militärische Notwendigkeit und Humanität' ('Military Necessity and Humanity'), an eloquent and experienced presentation of the argument that it was often necessary to be cruel to be kind, and that in war as it really was (and *ought* to be), military necessity could know no law.[16] Twenty years later, the German General Staff's official manual of guidance on *Kriegsbrauch im Landkriege* ('The Conduct of War on Land') repeated the same lessons; beginning with some brisk equations of humanitarianism with unprofessionalism, and of soft-heartedness with soft-headedness, it insisted throughout its practical passages that, however humane and generous German officers would usually wish to be, they must let no such considerations stand in the way of achieving military objects.[17]

Such works were well known to general readers of military books (for which, both professional and popular, there was evidently a flourishing market). How the international lawyers handled these matters was less noticed, but they too, of course, were exercised by them, and the two basic attitudes to military necessity may be seen in Westlake's criticism of Lueder. Lueder, a professor at Wurzburg, contributed the key military section to the weightiest German international law book of the epoch, Holtzendorff's four-volume *Handbuch des Völkerrechts*.[18] On every sensitive or unsettled point, he took the harder line; in some respects a harder line, indeed, than that taken ten years later by the *Kriegsbrauch im Landkriege*.[19] For so doing he was much censured, by no one more eloquently than Westlake, his counterpart at Cambridge. Of Lueder's insistent hard doctrine on military necessity, Westlake wrote that what it amounted to was

> 'that the true instructions to be given by a state to its generals are: "Succeed — by war according to its laws, if you can — but, at all events and in any way, succeed" ... Of conduct suitable to such instructions [it may] be expected that human nature will not fail to produce examples, but the business of doctrinal writers should be to check, and not to encourage it. Otherwise the most elementary restraints on war, which have been handed down from antiquity, are not safe.'[20]

To sum up Westlake's conclusion another way, it was not a matter of honesty or clarity of thought, but one of fundamental moral tendency, whether one said, 'These are the laws of civilised warfare and if you break them you must be prepared subsequently to show good cause why you did so', or 'These are the laws of war but you may break them whenever you think it militarily advantageous to do so'.

The argument through the principal part of this essay having acquired (perhaps because of my ignorance of Russian and other possibly comparable military practices) a somewhat anti-German appearance, it is peculiarly necessary to remark in conclusion that a very similar effect would result from a comparative examination of international law as the British preached and practised it.[21] Such comments, indeed, were made, and with great force, by the Germans themselves, once the First World War's propaganda campaigns got going. The British (though not the British only) found fault with the German's conduct of land war. The British conduct of war at sea upset the Germans (and, through at any rate the first half of the war, the bulk of neutral opinion likewise). If the German military tradition had bred an attitude to international laws and usages which reserved for the German army the right to dispense with them in the sacred and ultimate cause of national self-preservation, so had the British naval tradition evolved a patronising, selective approach to international law which, shorn of its idealist, internationalist *pax britannica* wool, meant that the Admiralty reserved the right to dispense with whatever international laws of war at sea did not ultimately suit British self-interest. Many and bitter were the comments which the Germans, as the current self-appointed representatives of neutral interests, made on the British in their self-appointed role of international moralists; comments sometimes based on ancient witticisms, like 'La droit internationale Britannique est la droit des canons', and ' "Britannia rules the waves" means that Britannia waives the rules'.

There was something in it! The parallels cannot be fully drawn out here. It may, however, be noted that the British had been as prominent in the formation of the international law of sea war as had the French and Germans, rival arbiters of land war niceties, in that domain. The law which the British had since the later seventeenth century enforced in respect of maritime neutrals (to whom Britain's continental foes of course looked for assistance in their overseas affairs) had always been thought offensive to them, and whenever they found enough collective strength to defy it they had done so: by military menace in the 'armed neutralities' of 1780 and 1800, more by organisation of (to use a loose but intelligible phrase) world public opinion in the 1856 Declaration of Paris and the 1909 Declaration of London, which brought to a finish business that had been ostentatiously begun at the second Hague Conference two years before. Yet within the Admiralty and inner British strategic planning circles it remained axiomatic that none of these apparent concessions to neutralist interests would be allowed to hinder the fullest necessary exercise of British naval supremacy, just as it had been understood that the concessions themselves were 'safe' ones, withdrawals from exposed positions which were no longer as vital as they formerly had been. When the First World War started, the way contraband lists were made up and blockade begun showed that the British, albeit restrained by regard to neutral (i.e. principally United States) susceptibilities, were no less ready than the Germans to justify stretchings of custom and infringements of the law (in so far as it was beyond dispute, which as a matter of fact it often was not) on the grounds of 'necessity'. The parallel in that case seems close and exact. The parallel appears also in respect of the law on requisitions, etc., which, as peoples likely to be occupied increasingly pointed out during the years before 1914, even after the 1907 Hague Conference left the prospective invader and occupier free, if he chose, to suck the occupied territory dry. If the first parallel tended, from the detached standpoint of 'world opinion', to make the Germans seem no worse than the British, this second one had the opposite tendency; and in so far as it was part of German self-respect to claim that they were at least frank about their military hardness, it invited their critics to remark that, in the matter of 'enemy private property', it was the British who were frank about their intention to seize it, and the Germans who were disingenuous.

In an even larger though looser way, through the second half of the war and during subsequent polemics, an affecting parallel was sketched in respect of the most 'innocent' of non-combatants, the women and children, sick, aged, etc., the arch-civilians of whom only remote morale sustaining functions could at most be predicated. The British, whose non-combatants of this kind could only be much hurt by bombardment and unannounced attacks on non-naval vessels, complained about German beastliness when shells and bombs came from sea and air onto British towns and when German torpedoes and mines sank British passenger ships. The Germans, whose counterpart non-combatants could only be much hurt by food shortages, complained about British beastliness when the naval blockade became as total as the British could make it, from 1916 onwards. To what extent food blockades and unrestricted sea warfare were legally justifiable, which they may have been *per se* and certainly could have been as reprisals, we shall not here enquire. Even when restricted to its legal terms and in the hands of an unusually lucid and readable international lawyer, such an argument remains a knotty one, as may be seen from Kalshoven's passages on the equivalent debate during the Second World War.[22] Nor is the international legal decision bound to be any more satisfying to the moral sense than the national, 'municipal' legal decision. International law develops slowly and piecemeal in the rear of international realities. To offer a notorious instance, the soldier who sights and kills an enemy non-combatant is *prima facie* guilty of an offence while the crew of the bomber who blindly unleash the means of killing hundreds of enemy non-combatants are not. This is a nonsense, but, given the natures of the international system and international law, a (temporarily) excusable one. The reasonable internationally minded man, while sympathising with the lawyer's predicament, may wish to work on a wider canvas and to hazard looser opinions. In particular he might contemplate the argument in defence of submarine warfare, that by its very nature the submarine had to be 'inhumane': it dared not show itself, it was almost pathetically vulnerable on the surface, it could carry neither prize crews to put aboard captured ships nor survivors of ships it sank. German apologetics harped on this theme, which is clearly analogous to that used in our own day to justify the use of guerrilla methods and 'terror' by 'minorities' and of torture by anyone. The question might nevertheless be thought to remain: in what historically long term and philosophically acceptable senses has a battle or a war been 'won' by means like that?

Notes

1. I.e. the Brussels Conference on the Rules of Military Warfare, 1874, and the Hague Conferences (on 'Peace and Disarmament') of 1899 and 1907. The first two resulted from Russian initiatives and the third was formally convened by Russia, though other powers were by then equally interested.
2. A detailed treatment of this subject would have to note, for example, the controversy over the British attempts to prevent food getting to France and her continental system during the 1793-1814 wars; and the awareness shown by, for example, Sherman and Moltke, of the nature of their military problem in mastering a nationally diffused enemy.
3. Their view of it is well expressed, with a vigour born of urgency, in the 1863 Instructions for the Government of the Armies of the United States in the Field, the work chiefly of the German-American jurist Franz Lieber. This document is especially interesting as an argued exposition of principles as well as a code of regulations.
4. I say 'from a European point of view' because American Civil War developments in land war, though very important to any comprehensive view of the subject, were, as a matter of fact, not much noticed in our debate; and I pass over the many European conflicts in which 'the people' had been involved (the Greek War of Independence, Italo-Austrian Wars, the Hungarian Insurgency of 1849, etc.) simply because they *were* passed over, so far as I can judge, in the grand and 'official' debate with which I am concerned. That they were so passed over suggests how strongly the debate's conductors were biased or blinded against recognition of the realities of armed conflict outside their exceptionally civilised circles.
5. This was, in siege situations, an ancient practice, a corrosive worm in the budding distinction between combatants and non-combatants. Militarist minds, characteristically contemptuous and ignorant of 'civilian' ones, have always tended to over-rate its effectiveness.

6. I have not gone deep enough to be able to judge whether this was because the Prussians felt more strongly about it than the Russians, who for sure were equally interested in it, or simply because circumstances pressed them to do most of the talking about it.

7. The final state of the international law on contributions and requisitions as established at the Hague, 1907, articles 49 to 53, though hedged about with good-sounding prohibitions and qualifications, in effect permitted the occupier to take anything in money, kind or services that he judged necessary for the army of occupation, so long as (art. 52) requisitions in kind and services were 'in proportion to the resources of the county'. This last qualification amounted to little in reality. The occupier was as much judge of what was 'proportionate' as of what his occupation needs were; he would pay for what it suited him to pay for, take what was more convenient to take; and all qualifications and prohibitions lapsed the moment he felt inclined to invoke 'military necessity', his right to punish, or his right of reprisal.

8. My grounds for saying that the Germans made more of it than any other powers are the sense of it as a German peculiarity conveyed by Westlake (*International Law, Part II: War*, Cambridge, 1907, p. 90) and Rolin (*Droit moderne de la guerre*, 3 vols., Brussels, 1920, I, pp. 372-3), and the impression gained from my own reading that they are right. J. M. Spaight, *War Rights on Land* (London, 1911, p. 334) points out that it occurs also in the 1877 *Manuel de droit international a l'usage des officiers*. His suggestion (on p. 335) that Lord Kitchener incorporated it into British practice in his governance of the Orange Free State is, considering the circumstances of 1900, unconvincing. I should dearly like to know to what extent the Russians used it. No explicit attention is paid to it by D. A. Graber, *The Development of the Law of Belligerent Occupation, 1863-1914* (New York, 1949).

9. Brand Whitlock, *Belgium under the German Occupation* (2 vols., London, 1919), I, p. 305.

10. PRO, FO 881/2542, Correspondence with General Horsford respecting the Conference at Brussels . . . 25 July-28 September 1874, pp. 84, 94 (my paraphrase).

11. See above, note 8.

12. Not that that brought much relief if occupation lasted long between the armistice and the final peace treaty. Danes (1864) and Frenchmen (1871) knew too well what that meant.

13. Colmar von der Goltz, *Das Volk in Waffen. The Nation in Arms*, trans. P. A. Ashworth. Fifth edition 1898; London, 1906, p. 468.

14. I must remark that I have not read enough French works to be sure where they stood on this matter. At the international conferences they certainly did not appear to side with the Germans. Presumably they were anxious not to. Westlake, *op. cit.*, pp. 115-7 equates with Lueder's teaching (see below, notes 18 and 20) that of Rivier, *Principes du droit des gens*.

15. Dated 'Berlin, 11 December 1880', its French translation may be found in *Revue de Droit International*, XIII (1881), pp. 79-82. The original is in Moltke's *Gesammelte Schriften und Denkwürdigkeiten* (Berlin, 1892-3), V, pp. 194-7.

16. His *Deutsche Rundschau* obituary notice (xv, 494-5) says he was son of the Hanoverian Hartmann who served under Wellington, and a cavalry commander in the wars of 1866 and 1870. J. W. Garner, *International Law and the World War* (2 vols., London, 1920, I, p. 278) quotes one Saint Yves (*Les Responsabilités de l'Allemagne*, p. 338) as saying that Hartmann's articles were written at official instigation to counter the soft line of Bluntschli, the 'greatest international jurist of the day' (J. Lorimer, *Institutes of the Laws of Nations*, 2 vols., Edinburgh, 1884, II, p. 188).

17. This 1902 work (originally no. 31 of the Great General Staff series *Kriegsgeschichtliche Einzelschriften*) was translated into French by Carpentier, 1904, and into English by J. H. Morgan as *The German War Book*, 1915. The extent to which its teaching seemed incompatible with the 1899 and 1907 Hague Rules was closely watched! The Hague Rules were in several respects gentler. Evidence of determination not to be held back by them is given by E. Stenzel, 'Uber die "Kriegsräson" des kaiserlichen deutschen Militärismus', in *Zeitschrift für Militärgeschichte*, IV (1965), p. 343.
18. Four vols., Berlin, 1899. Lueder's section fills Vol. IV, pp. 169-367. It is noteworthy that Lueder in 1874 won the Empress Augusta's prize for a history of humanity in warfare. Its tone was so hostile to the French that the Comité Internationale de la Croix Rouge, who had to manage its translation into the tongue of Geneva, asked him to revise it. In vain! ('Papiers Divers' in CICR Archives, box 21: Travaux, 1e série, 1863-76).
19. Thus Nys, *Le Droit International* (3 vols., Brussels, 1904), III, p. 204.
20. *International Law: Part II, War* (Cambridge, 1907), pp. 116-17. See further his *Collected Papers* . . . (ed. Oppenheim, Cambridge, 1914) ch. 11. On pp. 244-6 he gives a translation of the passages in Lueder he found most offensive.
21. Not to mention the faults found by the Germans (and practically everyone else) with the British conduct of their recent land war against the Boers. I am grateful to Dr John Röhl for reminding me of this, as well as for a multitude of other helpful comments on the typescript, most of which I have taken to heart.
22. F. Kalshoven, *Belligerent Reprisals* (Leyden, 1971).

NOTES ON CONTRIBUTORS

JOHN KEEGAN is a senior lecturer at The Royal Military Academy, Sandhurst, and has written extensively on problems connected with the First and Second World Wars.

RICHARD LUCKETT is Assistant Lecturer in English at Cambridge. His book on the Russian Civil War, *The White Generals*, was published in 1971.

DOUGLAS PORCH is a Lecturer at the University of Wales, Aberystwyth. His book, *Army and Revolution: France 1815-48*, was published in 1974.

ANDREW WHEATCROFT has written on the Austrian arms industry, and aspects of the Austro-Hungarian army. He edited *The Habsburg Empire* (London, 1971) and has lectured widely on nineteenth-century Austria.

VOLKER BERGHAHN is Professor of Modern History at the University of Warwick, and has published widely in German and English. His most recent work includes *The Tirpitz Plan* (1972) and *Germany and the Approach of War in 1914* (London, 1973).

CLIVE TREBILCOCK is Lecturer in Economic History at Cambridge. He has published numerous articles on the economic aspects of armaments, and his study of the British armaments industry is to be published shortly.

NORMAN STONE is Lecturer in History at Cambridge. He has written extensively on the Habsburg empire, and the mobilisation crisis of 1914. His book on *The Eastern Front, 1914-17* appeared in 1975.

GEOFFREY BEST is Professor of European History at the University of Sussex. Until January 1974, he was Richard Lodge Professor of History at Edinburgh University. His published work includes *Shaftesbury* (London, 1964), *Temporal Pillars* (Cambridge, 1964) and *Mid-Victorian Britain* (London, 1971).